Pt. Deendayal Upadhyaya's Roadmap for India

Pt. Deendayal Upadhyaya's Roadmap for India

Vivasvan Shastri

PRABHAT PRAKASHAN
ISO 9001: 2008 Publishers

Published by
PRABHAT PRAKASHAN
4/19 Asaf Ali Road,
New Delhi-110 002 (INDIA)
Tele: +91-11-23289777
E-mail: prabhatbooks@gmail.com

ISBN 978-93-5266-402-3
PT. DEENDAYAL UPADHYAYA'S ROADMAP FOR INDIA
by Vivasvan Shastri

Edition
First, 2018

Price
₹ 300.00 (Rupees Three Hundred only)

Printed at
R-Tech Offset Printers, Delhi

To my mother and motherland

तेरा वैभव अमर रहे माँ, हम दिन चार रहें न रहें

अनंतकुमार
ANANTHKUMAR
ಅನಂತಕುಮಾರ್

रसायन एवं उर्वरक तथा संसदीय कार्य
मंत्री भारत सरकार
MINISTER OF CHEMICALS &
FERTILIZER AND PARLIAMENTARY
AFFAIRS GOVERNMENT OF INDIA

सत्यमेव जयते

FOREWORD

If I must name one person, who has inspired lakhs and millions very silently but nevertheless very powerfully, it is undoubtedly Pt. Deendayal ji. His life span achieved so much in terms of vision and action, that it aptly presented a roadmap for Bharat and the world for years and even decades to come.

His focus on 'Integral Humanism' as an anchor point for our Political philosophy is highly relevant in today's time. Unless there is a focus on the last person of our society who needs help, the society doesn't succeed. His enunciation of interconnectedness among 4 different levels is indeed the need of the hour for the entire humanity – Vyashti (individual), Samashti (Society), Srushti (Nature) and Parameshti (divinity). When one sees this complementarity of these 4 levels, all the conflicts get resolved automatically. This approach not only is relevant for individuals, but also to nations (as vyashti) when compared to the whole set of countries taken as samashti. His views on 'Integral Humanism' tells us the opt repeated but little followed principle of 'Vasudhaiva Kutumbakam'.

I am glad that a simple rendering of profound philosophical views of Pt. Deendayal ji has been very nicely attempted by Vivasvan Shastri. I congratulate him for this effort and hope that this reaches many people all over the world, to make our planet a better place to live in.

(ANANTHKUMAR)

22 Nov., 2017

Office : Room No. 316, Shastri Bhawan, Dr. Rajendra Prasad Road, New Delhi-110001
Tel.: +91-11-23383559, 23386519 Fax : +91-11-23384020
Office : Room No. 15, Parliament House New Delhi-110001 Tel.: +91-11-23017780, 23017798, 23018729 Fax : +91-11-23792341
Residence : 26, Tughlak Crescent, New Delhi-110011 Tel.: +91-11-23794754, Fax : +91-11-23012791
Bengaluru Office : 15th Cross, 2nd Block, Jayanagar, South End Circle, Bengaluru-560011
Telefax : +91-80-26560286, 26571188 e-mail : ananthkumardelhioffice@gmail.com, ananth@ananth.org
Visit : www.ananth.org

Author's Note

The ideas, thoughts, and concepts conveyed in this book belong solely to Pandit Deendayal Upadhyaya. This book attempts to present a vision and a roadmap for the reconstruction of India. I have made an honest attempt to consolidate Pandit Deendayal's thoughts on R*raj-neeti* (politics), *Artha-neeti* (economics), *Samaj-shastra* (sociology), *Rashtra-neeti* (nation-building), and *Ekatma Manav Darhsan* (integral humanism) and present them in a concise manner.

The book also contains four important speeches of Pandit Deendayal from which his idea of India has been distilled.

Given the prevalent reading habits, I have made an attempt to present the thoughts and works of Pandit Deendayal in a manner such that the book can be read in two to three hours—the average time a reader would spend on social media platform, such as Facebook and WhatsApp, daily.

I hope that I have been able to do justice to the ideas of a *rishi* like Pandit Deendayal Upadhyaya. Any failure to do so is solely mine.

I hope this book goes on to inspire politicians, statesmen, social and cultural organizations to build an India as envisioned by Pandit Deendayal Upadhyaya.

Bharat Mata Ki Jai!
@VivaShastri

Contents

1
Early Years

In the history of the world, it would be rare to find a man who in his lifetime changes the destiny of a thousand-year-old civilization and yet remain virtually anonymous. In his short life that left a profound impact on generations to come, he earned no accolades, no Bharat Ratna, no Nobel Prize, but his works on raj-neeti (politics), artha-neeti (economics), rashtra-neeti (nation-building), and *samaj-shastra* (sociology) ended up shaping the destiny of the nation.

Pandit Deendayal Upadhyaya was born on 25 September 1916 in Chandrabhan village, not very far from Mathura. Panditji's father, Bhagwati Prasad, was a famous astrologer, and his mother, Rampyari, was a very religious-minded lady. As per Indian customs, a *janam kundali* or horoscope was prepared. An astrologer who read Panditji's horoscope predicted that he would go on to become a great scholar, thinker, and maybe even a leading politician.

As Deendayal turned two, the family was blessed with another son—Shiv Dayal. Six months later, Deendayal's father passed away. Deendayal went to live with his maternal grandfather, Chunnilal Shukla. When Deendayal was barely six years old, his mother too passed away. In a few years, death struck again. Deendayal lost his brother, Shiv Dayal. Deendayal was now orphaned and alone.

India's unique joint-family system provided Deendayal the social safety net; Deendayal was now taken care of by his maternal uncle and his family, who remained close to him till the last days of his life.

Under the guardianship, love, and care of his maternal uncle and aunt, Deendayal began to excel in academics. He went to high school in Sikar, from where he matriculated. Deendayal got the topmost rank in the Ajmer board exam and received a gold medal and scholarship from the Maharaja of Sikar. Deendayal again topped the intermediate exams at the Birla College of Pilani and went on to complete his BA (mathematics) from the Sanatan Dharma College at Kanpur in 1939.

For master's degree in English literature, he joined St John's College in Agra. Unfortunately, due to an illness in the family, he could not appear for the final year exams. Deendayal's maternal uncle encouraged him to take the provisional services exam. As always, Deendayal did very well in the exam but declined to join the services.

The struggle, tragedy, and accomplishments of his early life taught Deendayal a valuable lesson that would end up shaping his work and philosophy.

In India, when bad fortune hits you, the safety net of the extended family is always there for you. A strong nation is built on a foundation of strong families. This principle of a family being the fundamental building block of a society and the nation would guide his *raj-neeti*, *artha-neeti*, *samaj-shastra*, and *rashtra-neeti* for many decades to come.

Pandit Deendayal's life now took a turning point.

□

2
Sangha Shiksha

During his college years at Sanatan Dharma College in 1937, Deendayal became friends with Sunder Singh Bhandari and Balawant Mahashabde, who introduced him to the Rashtriya Swayamsevak Sangh (RSS). Deendayal met the founder of RSS, Dr. Keshav Hedgewar, at an RSS *shakha* and engaged with him in an intellectual discussion.

To understand Deendayal and the organizations that he went on to build during his lifetime, it's important to understand the Rashtriya Swayamsevak Sangh (RSS), its objectives, and its ways of working.

Dr. Keshav Baliram Hedgewar founded RSS on Vijaydashmi Day in 1925. Dr Hedgewar, who is popularly referred to as Doctorji, was once a member of the Congress Party. A good reader of history, Doctorji concluded that the Congress Party is a reactionary movement against the British with little vision on what to make of India post independence. For the Congress, independence was the final destination, but for Doctorji, it was just a means, or a precondition, for the development and reconstruction of India after a thousand years of slavery.

Doctorji analysed the last 1,000 years of slavery of India and felt that lack of organization was a fundamental flaw within the Indian society, leading to its successive defeats in the hands of invaders.

Doctorji outlined a four-stage roadmap for rebuilding the nation.

Stage 1: Organize society. Bring together people across the nation under a single banner.

Stage 2: Use culture as a binding glue. While religion, caste, and class divide, culture unites.

Stage 3: Develop leadership qualities. Transformation of a country begins with the transformation of one individual at a time.

Stage 4: Provide a compelling vision to strive for. The RSS prayer provides a glimpse of this vision, referred to as 'Param-vaibhavam'—i.e. for the nation to realize its potential and ultimate glory. Swami Vivekananda referred to this same vision as 'Bharat being a *Jagad Guru*'.

The means for executing to this roadmap is called *shakha*. A *shakha* is a daily meeting of members of the RSS who are called *swayamsevaks* (volunteers). The *shakha* aims to bring about all-round development of a *swayamsevak*—body, mind, intellect, and soul. *Shakha* provides a training ground to develop individuals who will be inspired to bring about change in the nation.

Some of the characteristics of an ideal *swayamsevak* as outlined by Madhav Golwalkar popularly called as Guruji, the second Sar-Sanchalak or President of the RSS, are:

1. **Character and conduct:** Guruji once remarked, 'Just like a coin, our life has two sides. One of these two sides is our personal character, which should be pure. The other side pertains to the nation and society; it implies restriction of our self-interest and joyful bending of our all efforts towards serving the interest of the nation without caring for our personal inconvenience. This is what is called as the national character and forms the other side. A person can be considered good if both the sides of his character like the two sides of a coin are good. If one side of the coin is worn, then even though the other side is good, it is considered as a bad coin.' An ideal *swayamsevak* should possess purity of character, both personal and national.

   On conduct, Guruji remarked, 'Doing good work requires earning the confidence of the people, people will put faith in us only when our conduct is pure. Our personal life should be unblemished that no one should even dream of suspecting us.'

2. **Discipline:** 'It is the coming together of little things in an organized manner that goes to make a great thing. Take care of the pence and the pounds will take care of themselves is an adage that is true to a letter in the molding of great characters. Great characters do not come up as ready-made products in a day. They are built silently and steadily, and their glorious heights scaled inch by inch and step by step.'
3. **Commitment, courage, and passion with purpose:** Transformation of a civilization which is thousands of years old and has spent hundreds of years under slavery is unlikely to happen in a lifetime. There will be many setbacks along the way. Commitment and courage to persevere against odds and opposition is needed, given the task at hand.
4. **Ability to win over others:** There is a saying that it is very easy to defeat someone but very hard to win someone. Non-egoist nature, cooperation and collaboration in place of conflict and competition, and sweet speeches are critical to win hearts and minds.
5. **Service and sacrifice:** Country first, society second, and self last. Personal and community interest always comes second to those of the nation. RSS believes in protecting the individuality of every *swayamsevak* and, at the same time, leveraging their strengths for the good of society. As a true *karma yogi*, every *swayamsevak* should be a man of action, contributing to the betterment of the community and the society he lives in.

On the auspicious day of *Makar Sankranti*, Deendayal took the RSS oath at its Kanpur *shakha*. Deendayal continued with his studies and joined the BT course in Prayag. In 1941, time had come for him to look for a job and settle down.

The 1940s was a turbulent time for India. The world was at war, and freedom for India was nowhere in sight. Partition on religious lines was a serious threat, and society was at the verge of disintegration. Deendayal decided to dedicate his life in the service of society and the nation. He believed this could be best achieved by working with the RSS. He decided not to take up a job and join the RSS. After attending a forty-day RSS training camp in Nagpur, Deendayal became a *pracharak*, or a full-time worker of the RSS.

In a letter written to his uncle, Deendayal remarked, 'God has blessed our family with some means. Can we not offer at least one of our members for the service of the nation? Having provided me with education, moral instruction and all sorts of qualifications, can you not turn me over to *samaj*, to which we owe so much?'

Life as a *pracharak* was that of *karma yogi*. You will hear many anecdotes on how Deendayal used to survive just on gram, take shelter in a shop, and walk in the rain. Deendayal washed his own clothes. Simplicity and frugality underlined the life of Deendayal.

When the RSS constitution was drafted, Deendayal's participation was substantial. He continued to work as a *pracharak* in Lakshmipur district of Uttar Pradesh till 1944 and then was given the responsibility of *sah-prant pracharak* of Uttar Pradesh, a responsibility he carried on till 1951.

During the 1940s, the author and the historian in Deendayal took birth. In 1947, a publisher by the name of Rashtra Dharma Prakashan was started, which published a magazine *Rashtra Dharma*, a weekly *Panchjanya*, and daily *Swadesh*. Deendayal edited *Panchjanya* and *Swadesh*. The editorial team included Atal Bihari Vajpayee, who would go on to be the Prime Minister of India.

Deendayal also went on to author two books: *Samrat Chandragupta* and *Jagat Guru Shankaracharya*, which were published in 1946 and 1947 respectively.

As a RSS *pracharak*, Deendayal continued to build and strengthen the organization at the grass roots level.

The period from 1937 to 1951 as a RSS *pracharak* would play a pivotal role in helping Deendayal launch a national alternative model of governance and development—a model that would continue to change the destiny of generations for decades to come.

□

3

One Country, One People, One Culture, One Nation

From tomorrow we shall be free from the slavery of British rule but the partition of India is also to take place at midnight today. Therefore, tomorrow will be the day of rejoicing as also a day of sorrow.

— Mahatma Gandhi, 14 August 1947

A movement called the Congress, formed and taken forward by the likes of Dadabhai Naoroji, Lokmanya Tilak, Lala Lajpatrai, and many others, would also change overnight from being a movement to a political party. A political party that would take over the reins from the British. Mahatma Gandhi had advocated that the Congress transform itself into a social service organization and serve the rural India in the name of Lok Sevak Sangh.

But then power is intoxicating. Jawaharlal Nehru went on to become the first Prime Minister of India. Nehru was chosen over a popular Sardar Patel.

Congress as a movement had one goal—liberation from the British. Very little was articulated about what to do post independence. Freedom in the true sense is not only political but includes social, economic, and cultural freedom as well.

1,000 years of slavery had left India not only impoverished but also socially fragmented. A roadmap was required to reconstruct India—a roadmap that would chart a future course based on timeless Indian ethos, values, and culture. It was expected that the

Congress would work out a plan to rebuild India.

Congress as a movement was a collection of various forces—nationalist, Gandhian, and socialist/communist. After assuming the form of a political party, these forces began to fight within themselves to be the primary ideology of the Congress Party.

The first casualty was the Gandhian thinking. Gandhiji was assassinated soon after independence in 1948. Nehru blamed the nationalist forces for the assassination. He went on to ban the RSS and Hindu Mahasabha. Sardar Patel was also not spared, and a parliamentary inquiry was ordered to check if the Gandhiji was provided adequate security.

Post trial and investigation, the nationalist forces were cleared by the judiciary. Sardar Patel passed a resolution in the Congress Working Committee, requesting RSS to join with the Congress. Fearing that such a move would strengthen Sardar Patel, Nehru negated the resolution. Sardar Patel too did not live long. The two foundational pillars of the Congress, Mahatma Gandhi and Sardar Patel, left in quick succession, leaving a vacuum—political and ideological. Nehru's views now prevailed over the party and the nation.

Nehru attempted to fill this vacuum with the import of two ideas from Europe—secularism and socialism.

Secularism took birth in Europe as the first reactionary movement to balance the excessive involvement of the Church in all the affairs of the State and public life. Power of the Pope made way for the power of monarchs. This separation of the Church and State was referred to as secularism.

Monarchy gave way to democracy, which ushered in the Industrial Revolution. With the success of the Industrial Revolution, power now shifted to the hands of the few who had access to capital. These capitalists used their leverage to maximize their gains at the cost of labour and natural resources. Labour felt helpless, exploited, and without much hope. This gave birth to socialism.

Both secularism and socialism were reactionary movements to local problems in specific countries.

India in 1947 was poor and divided—a primarily agrarian economy which was communally divided. Nehru borrowed and imposed the Russian-styled model of development on a poor agricultural economy. The Russian model called for centralized planning, centralized control, massive state-owned factories, and collective farming. A human was reduced to a mere economic entity.

The model centralized all resources and approving powers with a chosen few government officials. These officials would then dictate how every part of India would develop. This centralization and the resulting *licence raj* laid the foundation of corruption, which would only blossom for many decades to come.

Centralization of all planning and decision making resulted in a totalitarian regime. The states and people at large were made dependent on the benevolence of a single party and an individual in particular.

Large-scale state-owned factories required massive capital. As India lacked capital on its own, the only solution was to take on debt from foreign countries. Large-scale factories require not only large amounts of capital but also a huge amount of natural resources for production. The produced goods had a limited domestic market, given the low purchasing power of the population at large. Import and imposition of the Russian socialist model on India resulted in the dumping of legacy-antiquated technology from abroad in India at a hefty premium. This stifled local research and development and resulted in India being dependent on foreign countries even for its own defence.

. The agrarian population of India felt disconnected with this alien model of governance and development. One would wonder why a five-thousand-year-old civilization could not find anything of its own despite once being a leader in the global economy and had to borrow an alien model of governance and development.

What is freedom if one cannot be economically free? Independence only meant changing the *raj* from the *British raj* to *Congress's licence raj*. The goodwill that the Congress had now began to evaporate.

Partition and creation of Pakistan did not result in peace. Partition gave birth to pogroms. The Noakhali genocide in 1946 saw massacres, rapes, abductions, and forced conversion of Hindus in what is now Bangladesh. The pogroms peaked in 1950. The Barisal riot that began with attacks on *Janmashtami* processions peaked on *Vijayadashami* when homes of Hindus were set on fire. Lakhs of refuges now made way for India.

India and Indians expected Nehru to leverage his global stature to intervene. Intervene he did, but the intervention resulted in the Nehru-Liaquat Pact of 1950. The pact did little to get justice for the victims who had taken refuge in India but allowed them the freedom to go back unmolested to dispose their property, get back abducted women, etc.

Need was now felt for an alternative to the Congress Party—an alternative that could:

a. Provide a model of governance and development based on Indian ethos and values.
b. Use culture as a glue to unify India.
c. Bring about social freedom by addressing social issues.
d. Secure India on all fronts.

When the Congress Party was virtually unchallenged from the *panchayat* to the parliament, hope arose in form of Dr. Shyama Prasad Mukherjee.

Dr. Mukherjee was at age thirty-three, the youngest Vice Chancellor of the Calcutta University. He joined the Hindu Mahasabha in 1939 and was elected its president in 1944. A close aide of Veer Savarkar, Dr. Mukherjee was an ardent devotee of Shri Aurobindo. Mother (Aurobindo's successor) believed that Dr. Mukherjee would be the rejuvenator of Indian nationalism and the builder of a new India.

Dr. Mukherjee was inducted into India's first cabinet at the behest of Mahatma Gandhi. He served as India's first Minister of industry and supply.

Dr. Mukherjee was at the odds with policy of Nehru to import and impose foreign models of development and governance. The final straw was the Nehru–Liaquat Pact, where—in the name of secularism—justice was denied to the Hindu minorities who were victims of a well-documented pogrom. On 6 April 1950, Dr. Mukherjee resigned from the cabinet and began his search to build a national alternative to the Congress, an alternative that would provide a roadmap for the rebuilding of India in tune with its ethos and culture.

Dr. Mukherjee consulted Guruji Golwalkar and sought his help. Guruji Golwalkar clarified that the RSS was a social and cultural organization. At best, RSS could provide a few volunteers to help Dr. Mukherjee to build a nationalist political alternative. One of the volunteers assigned to the task was Pandit Deendayal Upadhyaya.

In his speech at Jaunpur, Shri Guruji remarked, 'Deendayal Ji has not the slightest inclination to join politics. In past years he asked me several times "This is a nasty affair in which you have placed me. Permit me gain to do work of a *Pracharak.*" I said "Whom else can I put into this nasty affair?" Only a man with such deep and unfaltering faith in organization work can remain in this nasty affair and still be unaffected by it, he only can clean it up. None else can do it.'

The new nationalist political alternative was named Bharatiya Jan Sangh, or simply Jan Sangh. On 21 October 1951, Jan Sangh was launched as a political party with a oil *diya* as its symbol. Dr. Mukherjee was its president, and Pandit Deendayal was the general secretary of Uttar Pradesh branch and later became the general secretary at the all-India level.

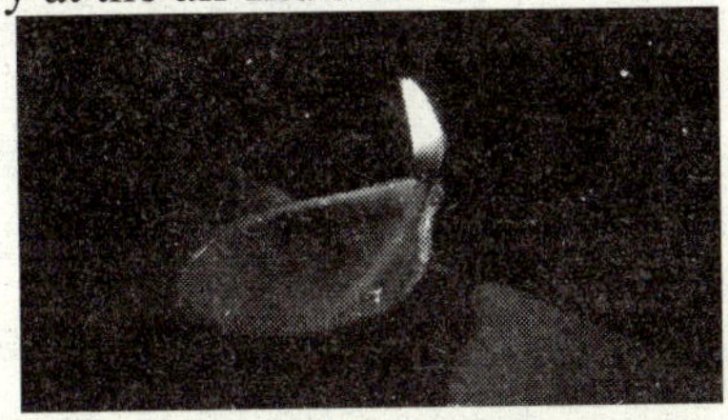

Diya: Election symbol of the Jan Sangh.

Every political party needs an ideology, organization, cadre, and a leader. Deendayal would play a pivotal role in defining the ideology of the Jan Sangh, building an organization, organizing and training its cadres, and one day being its leader.

In the Indian general election of 1951-52, Dr. Mukherjee and Pandit Deendayal went on to fight their first election as Jan Sangh. They secured 3.06 per cent of that national vote and bagged three seats. Based on the votes polled, the Jan Sangh acquired the status of a national party. Given what the Jan Sangh had managed to achieve in such a short span of time, Shyama Prasad Mukherjee had then famously remarked, 'If I could get two more Deendayals, I can change the political map of India.' Little did Shyama Prasad Mukherjee realize then that Deendayal would create an organization, national base of cadres, and an ideology that would indeed change the political map of India for decades to come.

As India celebrated its first democratic election as a republic, trouble had begun to brew on the Kashmir front. In 1947, Maharaja Hari Singh had signed the Instrument of Accession with India. This treaty was similar to the ones signed by the other states which joined the Union of India. However, Jawaharlal Nehru came under the influence of Sheikh Abdullah, president of the National Conference Party, which was formerly known as the Kashmir Muslim Conference. Sheikh Abdullah believed in the abolishment of monarchy, which was regarded as the principal backer of the feudal system prevailing in Jammu and Kashmir. Under the influence of Sheikh Abdullah, Nehru introduced Article 370 in the Indian Constitution, which gave special status to the state of Jammu and Kashmir.

Under Article 370, the people of Jammu and Kashmir via their elected representatives would:

a. Need to endorse accession to India (this led to later demands for a plebiscite).
b. Determine their own constitution.
c. Determine the jurisdiction of the Union of India.

The 1952 Delhi Agreement between Nehru and Sheikh Abdullah was a follow-up to Article 370. The 1952 agreement approved the accession to India but under some special terms:

1. Jammu and Kashmir would have its own separate constitution and flag.
2. Any Indian, including the president of India, would need a permit to enter the state.
3. Monarchy would be replaced by a constituent assembly, which would be elected every five years.

4. Fundamental rights guaranteed by the Constitution of India would not be applicable when it came to land reforms. This meant that no non-Kashmiri could buy land in the state.
5. J&K Assembly had the power to define rights and privileges of local residents.
6. Jurisdiction of the Supreme Court of India would be limited as regards to Kashmir.

The 1952 Delhi Agreement should have meant that Article 370 was no longer required and should be scrapped. However, Nehru decided to keep both Article 370 and the 1952 Delhi Agreement in play. This has led to demands from separatists even today asking for plebiscite and for full autonomy.

Shyama Prasad Mukherjee termed this the Balkanization of India, which could lead to its third partition. To prevent another partition, Jan Sangh launched a movement.

Lal Krishna Advaniji's blog vividly captures the movement and the tragic end of Shyama Prasad Mukherjee.

"In December 1952, the first all-India session of the Jana Sangh was held at Kanpur. It was at this conclave that Dr. Mukherjee gave a call to the country for the complete integration of Jammu and Kashmir state into the Indian Union. The call was summed up in a powerful slogan: '*Ek desh mein, Do Vidhan, Do Pradhan, Do Nishan Nahin Chalenge, Nahin Chalenge.*' (Ours is one country, we cannot have two constitutions, two presidents, two flags).

The Kanpur session ended with a resolve: to launch a countrywide movement for the full integration of J&K state into the union.

The movement was preceded by Dr. Mukherjee's correspondence with Prime Minister Pandit Nehru on this issue of J&K's full integration.

This was followed up by Dr. Shyama Prasad undertaking a countrywide tour on this issue. In this tour, he was accompanied by Shri Atal Bihari Vajpayee.

I was in Kota, Rajasthan, in those days. I can never forget meeting these two great stalwarts at the Kota railway station when the two were passing through Kota Junction.

The J&K government had decreed that any visitor to the state would be permitted entry only if he secured a permit from the state government. Dr. Mukherjee felt that this order of the state government was a violation of the Indian Constitution, so he decided that he himself would lead from the front the movement he had given a call for by defying the entry-permit order.

Dr. Mukherjee left Delhi for his Kashmir destination on 8 May 1953 by a passenger train carrying him and his entourage into Punjab. Throughout Punjab, it was a sea of humanity that accosted him everywhere.

His last stop was at the border check-post in Madhopur on the Ravi River, one of the great five rivers of Punjab, marking the boundary between Punjab and J&K. The day of his entry into this state was 10 May 1953. There was a road bridge across the Ravi. The boundary between the two states was supposed to be at the midpoint of this Madhopur bridge.

When the jeep carrying Dr. Mukherjee reached the centre point of the bridge, they found a posse of J and K police blocking the road. The Superintendent of Police, Kathua (J&K state), handed Dr. Mukherjee an order signed by the Chief Secretary of the state banning Dr. Mukherjee's entry into the state. 'But I am determined to go into the State,' Dr. Mukherjee declared.

Thereupon, the police officer took out an order of arrest under the Public Safety Act and took Dr. Mukherjee into custody. Vaidya Guru Dutt and Tekchand were two colleagues in the group who had been assigned the duty of accompanying Dr. Mukherjee when he was arrested. These two also courted arrest.

Dr. Mukherjee then spoke to Atalji and asked him to go back and convey to the people of the India that Dr. Mukherjee had defied the prohibitory orders and entered Jammu and Kashmir without a permit, though as a prisoner.

The place at which Dr Shyama Prasad was incarcerated was a small house near Nishat Bagh far away from Srinagar City. This house was converted into a sub-jail".

On 23 June 1953, the whole country was shocked to learn that after a brief illness at his place of detention, Dr. Mukherjee was shifted to the state hospital about ten miles away, where he had breathed his last.

Many believe Shyama Prasad Mukherjee was assassinated. He was administered penicillin even though he was allergic to it.

On hearing of her son's untimely death, Dr. Mukherjee's mother Jogamaya Debi exclaimed: 'Proudly do I feel that the loss of my son is a loss to Mother India!'

The untimely death of Shyama Prasad Mukherjee thrust Pandit Deendayal Upadhyaya into the into the role of a leader. Deendayal would go on to build an ideology, organization, and cadre around the ethos of 'One Nation, One People, One Culture, One Nation', a cause for which Shyama Prasad Mukherjee paid the ultimate price.

The leader and ideologue in Deendayal would now emerge.

□

4

Raj-Neeti

The purpose of politics is not to acquire power but to bring about social and economic changes in a peaceful manner.

Philosophy and Ideology

Political decisions and policy cannot be driven only by populist short-term goals but should be based on a philosophy that understands the social and economic situation within a country.

Based on this philosophy, a political party formulates its ideology. An ideology presents a political party's point of view on how it plans to bring about economic and social changes in the country. Any political party without a philosophy and an ideology only has the intent to capture power at all costs. This will result in corruption, and the party will be forced to indulge in vote bank politics and take recourse to actions which will only weaken a nation.

Deendayal understood this very well and, hence, started with defining the philosophy of the Jan Sangh, which would be the foundation on which its ideology, organization, cadre, and leaders will be developed.

The Jan Sangh philosophy can be articulated using the following principles:

1. *All actions should be based on dharma:* Dharma here is not a religion but the universal force that balances and sustains life. Any change (social or economic) which is not based on dharma will be short-lived and may end up doing more harm than good.
2. *Dedication to culture:* Culture is the foundation of national unity in India. Where religion and caste divides,

culture unites. The soul of a nation is its culture. Indian nationalism is based on our culture. Culture refers to our way of life or lifestyle that has sustained us for thousands of years. It is said that the best way to destroy a nation is to contaminate its culture. The political ideology of any party has to be in tune with the cultural ethos of the nation. Imported ideologies when forced on a population will never work. As Swami Vivekananda said, 'Imitation is not civilization.'

3. *Integral approach of development:* Our thinking and way of life has always been integral in nature. Development of individuals and societies are interlinked. The development of one cannot be at the cost of another. In the same breadth, the needs of the man need to be balanced with the available natural resources. Man is not a political or an economic entity alone; man is a social entity as well. Development of individuals should lead to the all-round development of society and nation.
4. *Transformation of a country begins with an individual:* There will be no magic formula to transform a nation. Transformation begins with the development of individuals. The purpose of politics is to create a social and economic environment which leads to the development of individuals. Perfection of a society can be judged from the perfection of its individuals.
5. *All-round development of individuals:* As man has more than just economic needs, the development of an individual should be on all fronts—economic and social. Policies and programmes of a political party should aim to provide a life of dignity for every individual. This principle is in sync with the four *purusharthas*—*artha*, *kama*, dharma, and moksha. Artha: policies should ensure total employment which generates adequate income for an individual and his family. Kama: production and distribution of goods and services should be adequate to meet the needs and desires of an individual. Dharma:

balance the needs of individuals with those of the society, and leverage natural resources in a sustainable way. It is only when the policies and programmes of the party address *artha* and *kama* using dharma can an individual strive towards realizing his or her own potential—i.e. moksha.

6. *Focus on duties:* Politics should be conducted in a way that an individual is made aware of his or her duties towards fellow citizens, society, and the nation at large. Politics based on rights or entitlements leads to confrontation, competition, and conflict. When individuals discharge their duties first and then talk about rights, it creates collaboration, cooperation, and accelerated development of the society and the nation. One's rights should not be detrimental to the interests of other but should be complementary in nature.
7. *Commitment to democracy:* Democracy, in the truest sense, is not limited to politics. True democracy extends to the economic and social sphere as well. Democracy means decentralization—i.e. power is not vested in a single group or organization but is derived from the population at large. The goal of democracy is to develop the nation by developing individuals.
8. *Freedom is indivisible:* Freedom knows no boundaries. A prerequisite to development is total freedom. An individual needs to be free politically, economically, and socially to realize his or her potential. If a nation is not economically free, then it will always be at the mercy of other nations. Social freedom refers to the ability to realize one's potential without any prejudice or imposed constraints.
9. *Diversity and non-discrimination:* Policies and programmes of a party should be for the benefit of every citizen. Policies only benefitting certain groups at the cost of others will result in vote bank politics. Differences should be respected and accepted and not only tolerated.

10. *Antyodaya:* Criteria of development should be measured and judged by looking at the man at the lowest rung of the ladder. All policies and programmes should be designed keeping in mind the man at the lowest rung of the ladder.

The above outlined philosophy of the Jan Sangh developed by Deendayal provided a set of timeless principles on which the Jan Sangh designed its policies and programmes. These principles continue to inspire, guide, and motivate young political leaders even today.

These timeless principles are derived from the way of life of a civilization which is thousands of years old and are rooted in its cultural ethos. This timeless way of life is also referred to as Hinduness.

Party of Cadres

Cadres form the lifeblood of a political organization. The cadres take and explain the ideology, policies, and programmes of the party to the people. They also put forth the aspirations, hopes, and needs of the people to the organization. Hence, developing cadres is critical to the growth of a political party, and Deendayal put a lot of effort and emphasis on developing cadres.

An ideal party worker should have malice against none and should be a friend, teacher, and well-wisher of the people. A party worker should also rise above caste and community considerations.

Conduct of the cadre should be such that an opponent today becomes a voter tomorrow, a voter tomorrow should become a party member day after tomorrow, and a member should transform into a full-time member the next day.

Deendayal's idea was that a worker should develop into a leader who is always in touch with the people. A party cadre should be one who is committed to the people, to the party, to principles, and above all, to the nation.

A party should not be merely a collection of people who have come together to aspire for power, but they should have come together due to their shared beliefs and principles and a shared goal for the nation.

Deendayal believed that politics can be practised without aspiring for power, but such a practice requires discipline, dedication, and devotion. Discipline is critical as only a disciplined party can provide a disciplined administration.

Discipline is not merely the following of certain rules; discipline is self-inspired and provides the will power to sacrifice individual needs for the greater good. An ideal worker should have purpose to serve the people, passion to propagate the party's ideology, policies, and programmes, and persistence to build a national alternative.

Deendayal also defined a code of conduct for the workers:

1. Nation first, party second, self last.
2. Be committed to party principles, policies, and programmes.
3. Service of the people: politics is just a means a serve the people.

To sum it up, Deendayal wanted the cadres of the Jan Sangh to practise the politics of humanism in place of politics of power.

Fighting Elections

During Deendayal's lifetime, the Jan Sangh fought four elections, and in every outing, both the votes polled by the Jan Sangh and the seats won increased dramatically from three in 1952 to thirty-five in 1967. Deendayal's goal was to provide a political alternative to the Congress, and he built a political alternative using the following principles:

1. *Goal of elections:* The goal of every election campaign is to educate the people and create awareness of a party's policies and programmes. Towards this end, the party should attempt to contest the maximum number of seats and should attempt to win the maximum number of votes. Contesting every election with the maximum number of candidates is the best way to convey a party's ideology to the people. Both seats and votes have their importance. Even if an election is lost, the number of votes cast in favour could be useful in the planning for future policies. Every vote counts as the voter today is a party member tomorrow.
2. *Selection of candidates:* A candidate is the one who has worked in the constituency, who can give vent to people's

aspirations, and who can effectively express people's sentiments in the legislature. The candidate must dedicate his life to the service of the people and has to work single-mindedly for the party. Selection of candidates should not be on caste or community considerations. Qualification of a candidate should be the only consideration. Deendayal himself contested and lost an election but refused to make an appeal on the basis of caste/community lines.

3. *Election alliances:* Electoral adjustments in terms of sharing seats can be done for tactical gains. However, forming joint fronts should be limited as it prevents the growth of the party.
4. National unity should never be sacrificed at the altar of politics. One may contest an election, but all political parties need to work together post election for national interest.
5. *Funding:* Funding should only be taken from people who believe in and support the party's ideology, policies, and principles. For party-funding, Deendayal preferred the RSS method of *Guru Dakshina*—i.e. voluntary contributions from members on a regular basis.
6. *Propaganda and publicity:* Party-campaigning should be positive in nature. Rather than attacking other political parties, focus should be on the positive aspects of the policies and programme of the party. Rather than wasting energy in countering negative propaganda, focus should be on communicating positive ideals and plans. *Antyodaya*, or the man at the lowest rung, is the God of democracy, and all effort should be made to reach out to him to convey the ideology, policy, and programmes of the party. Cordial relations should be maintained with all political parties.

When in Opposition

During his lifetime, Deendayal also expressed his thoughts on how a political party should conduct itself when it is not in power.

1. *Sharpened social sensitivity:* When in opposition, the party should maintain connection with the people at all times. The opposition party should effectively place before the government the problems faced by the people and also work with the government in resolving the problems.
2. *Protect democracy:* The opposition party should ensure that the fundamental rights of the people are not violated at any time. Should these rights get violated, the opposition party should fight on behalf of the people for the restoration of their rights. It was this principle that inspired Jan Sangh to take on the government post the imposition of emergency and motivated them to fight tooth and nail till the emergency was withdrawn.
3. *Agitations and oppositions:* It is the right of the opposition party to oppose the administration when the voices of the people are not heard by the government or the government acts in a manner which is detrimental to national interest. The ideal model would be for both the government and the opposition parties to work together to ensure that people's grievances are understood and addressed. If the government fails to listen or understand the grievances of the people, the opposition has the right to launch movements. But these movements should at no time lead to anarchy or harm national interest. Opposition for the sake of opposition is against the interest of the people and the nation. An enemy's enemy is not your friend. At all times, there should only be one consideration—national interest.
4. *Fight corruption:* For a nation like India with limited capital resources, corruption is the biggest barrier to development. It is the duty of every party to check corruption and launch movements when necessary for the eradication of corruption.
5. *Effective political force:* Every opposition party should strive to provide a viable alternative to the administration.

Every policy and programme of the opposition party should be objective and from the national point of view. Blind opposition or agitation for the sake of agitation should not be the primary driver. Provocative or intemperate language should be avoided during political discourse. When in national interest, opposition parties should work with the administration for the larger good of the people.

Deendayal always put the nation's interest first. During the 1961 Chinese aggression, the farmer's agitation in Uttar Pradesh was unconditionally withdrawn. It is also the opposition party's responsibility to safeguard national interests.

Coalition Governments

Elections may throw up results wherein no single political party can form a government on its own. As there can be no vacuum in governance, a coalition or a multiparty government may be a necessity. Based on Deendayalji's writings and actions during the time, the following principles can be derived:

1. *No governance vacuum:* In the absence of a government, the people and nation will suffer. Also, not forming a government will be tantamount to ignoring the vote and mandate of the people. It will go against the ideals of democracy if no government is attempted to be formed post elections. Hence, a coalition government may be a necessity.
2. *Common programme:* Multiparty governments should be formed on the basis of a commonly agreed programme for governance. The common programme should not go against the stated ideology, policies, and programmes of the party.
3. *Continuance in coalition governments:* Continue to remain in multiparty government as long as it is feasible to serve the people and society.
4. *Independence:* Even when in a coalition government, the party should retain its independence to propagate its policies and programmes to the people. The party should continue to function as an independent parliamentary party in line with the party's constitution.

After the first general elections, 77 non-Congress members in a 160-member assembly had a formed a group in the Rajasthan assembly called Samyukta Vidhayak Sangh. Seven members of this group belonged to the Jan Sangh. Jan Sangh had then supported the policy that the ownership of the farm must be with the tiller. Five out of the seven members had then rebelled and refused to follow the party line. Deendayal immediately took action against the group of five. This is a big move given the small number of legislators Jan Sangh had at that time. Of the two remaining, one was Bhairon Singh Shekhawat, who went to become the Chief Minister of Rajasthan one day.

When in Power

The only objective of acquiring power through politics should be to serve the people. Power is to be used for the country's good and not for the party's good. There is no greater evil than power abused. Every vote polled is a mandate to translate the hopes and aspirations of the people into action. Deendayal gave the example of *Bhagwan* Shree Krishna. He fought a war and won it not for himself but for *dharma*. Thus, after fighting and winning an election, the power that is acquired has to be used for the greater good of the people, society, nation, and the world at large.

A politician thinks of the next election, but a statesman thinks of the next generation. When in power, the party should change gears from practising *raj-neeti* to *rashtra-neeti*. *Artha-neeti* and *samaj-shastra* are two important pillars of *rashtra-neeti*. The following chapters will attempt to describe Deendayal's thoughts on the same. □

5
Artha-Neeti

The purpose of any economic policy is to provide a life of dignity to every human being.

Any policy should always take into account the historical, social, and the economic environment of a nation. A policy which is not in tune with the social and cultural ethos of a nation is bound to fail. One wonders why a nation such as India, which has abundance of labour and natural resources, struggles to come out of poverty even after six decades of independence. The answer lies in the fact that economic models imported from outside are thrust on the nation without any consideration.

The focal point of any policy should be an individual and his family. Every human being aspires for a life of dignity. Dignity of life means having an environment and opportunities such that a human being can meet all of his or her basic needs and wants. Per Hindu philosophy, there are four goals in a life—*artha*, *kama*, *dharma*, and *moksha*.

At the most basic level of needs, we have *artha* and *kama*. Every human being has basic needs and wants. To meet one's needs and wants (*kama*), everyone needs money (*artha*). In the *abhav*, or paucity of money, where one cannot even meet their basic needs, it is difficult to expect them to follow *dharma*. Excess of money, or *prabhav*, leads to greed and the ultimate degradation of man and society.

Hence, the first goal of any economic policy is to provide total employment. Every able-bodied human being must be provided education and skills by society to meet their basic needs and wants. Those who are unable to (e.g. sick and the elderly) should be taken care of by society.

An individual and society are integrated to an extent that the society provides the education, skills, and job opportunities, and the individual in turn uses the money he or she has earned to take care of himself and contribute back to the society. This is meeting one's needs of *artha* and *kama* in line with *dharma*.

An economic policy should drive the use of *artha* and *kama* in line with *dharma* so that both the society and the individual are well placed to realize their own potential (i.e. *moksha*). Any job that does not provide an expression for the soul is, in fact, torture.

Before we define the broad parameters of a viable economic policy for Bharat, one must first understand its history as well as social and economic environment.

Bharat is a land that is blessed with plenty of people (labour) and abundance of natural resources (raw materials), but after a thousand years of slavery, we are left with very little capital. Under slavery, raw materials from Bharat were taken away for a pittance, and factory-made output was sold back at a premium. Lack of education and skill development has left the nation with fewer able-bodied citizens who can meet their basic needs.

Bharat is primarily an agrarian economy due to good weather and the abundance of natural resources that support the cultivation of crops all throughout the year. Agriculture is also the biggest provider of employment in Bharat.

Bharat is also a land where diversity is celebrated. Hinduism provides every human being with a roadmap and a set of tools to realize their potential. Realizing one's potential, or self-realization, is equated with attaining oneness with God. Hence, freedom, creativity, and respect for diversity are in the DNA of every Hindu.

Man is not alone but coexists with other men and things like plants, animals, and nature. A citizen of Bharat is also very integrated—he identifies himself with his family, society, and the world at large. This integrated mindset often motivates an individual to take care of not only himself but also his family and society. In every Indian family, there are individuals who have made personal sacrifices for the greater good of the family. There are families which have made sacrifices for the greater good of the society. This integrated bond is created by a sense of duty. It is very common to see people going out of their way to help a stranger. This integrated mindset means that any economic policy should address not only an individual but his family as well. In Bharat, taking care of one's own is not the responsibility of the government but that of every individual.

Hence, Bharat needs an economic policy which:

1. Optimizes the use of labour and natural resources with minimum capital.
2. Aaddresses its unique cultural needs of an integrated but diverse society.
3. Empowers every individual to a life of dignity and helps them realize their potential.

Let's measure how the imported models of capitalism and socialism fare with respect to the needs of Bharat.

Capitalism

Capitalism is based on the idea of an economic man. Individualism, or the drive to maximize one's own desires, drives an economic man. The model works on the jungle law of the survival of the fittest—i.e. to maximize one's own needs, one needs to compete with other human beings and exploit nature to the fullest.

A capitalist model requires access to capital. Those who have money make more money. Those without money need to work for someone with capital to make their ends meet. With access to capital and labour, a capitalist seeks to maximize his profits. Thus, with more money (*artha*), one can maximize one's desires (*kama*). There is no *dharma* to balance one's needs with those of others—be it the family, the nation, or the world at large. Gratifying one's desires is more important than realizing one's potential (*moksha*).

This model is widely adopted by Western countries which have access to capital. Focusing on the individual alone leads to the disintegration of the family system. Family itself is an optional institution, for it comes in the way to gratifying one's desires to the fullest.

The drive to maximize one's desires leaves individuals in debt. The duty of providing social security has been moved from the family to the state. With no family savings and with the responsibility to provide social security, countries are in huge debts. Greece is a classic case in point, but others are not far away.

As capitalism needs access to capital, it is not ideally suited for a nation like India, which lacks capital. Capitalism puts an individual's need above his family. Capitalism is competitive and not integrated in approach—one can only win at the cost of others. Hence, it is not in tune with the cultural ethos of Bharat. Any individual in a capitalist model is always fighting for survival against other and has little time to realize his potential.

Capitalism also results in centralization. Those with capital are free to exploit the rest—be it labour or natural resources. Capitalists monopolize the means of production and distribution. In addition, they leverage their money power to drive up consumption habits with the use of advertisements.

This centralization is nothing but a loss of freedom, which often results in exploitation. Capitalism often pays lip service to respecting diversity, for it is optional only if it helps in maximizing one's profit. Against this exploitation rises the movement of socialism.

Socialism

Socialism is not much different from capitalism. Instead of the capitalists, the capital and means of production and distribution are centralized in the state. In socialism too, man is a mere economic entity. As long as the basic needs are met, there is nothing more that a man could wish for.

Socialism believes that every citizen has the same needs as that of any other. This goes against the grain of diversity. Socialism is also against the institution of marriage and family and believes in people living in communes. A citizen loses identity in socialism and is left as a mere cog in the giant machinery of state.

Political, economic, and cultural freedom is lost to the politburo, which is dictatorial in nature. In theory, it was believed that this dictatorial politburo would be temporary in nature. History has shown that the dictatorship becomes a permanent feature.

All economic planning and activities are centralized. State-owned enterprises drive virtually all economic planning by leveraging the capital and labour of the people. The value created by any economic activity in a socialist state is owned by the state, which then decides on how to distribute it based on its needs.

Socialism is a battle between the freedom of individuals and the needs of society. Under socialism, an individual has no right to property and is reduced to a provider of labour. For a life of dignity, a human being is at the mercy of the state and its policies. Socialism is at odds with the Indian cultural ethos which believes in diversity, integrated outlook, and the freedom of every citizen to realize his or her own potential.

As seen, both the models of capitalism and socialism are ill-suited for a nation like Bharat. Sadly, a cocktail of both has been deployed from time to time, which has resulted in millions remaining poor for decades.

As India adopted the massive path of centralization that was preached by capitalism and socialism, India had to borrow huge amounts of capital and technology from foreign countries. Foreign investments came with conditions attached. These conditions cost India its freedom. Case in point is the devaluation of rupee by 35 per cent in a single day at the insistence of foreign powers.

Lack of focus on agriculture further meant that the country was dependent on foreign powers even to meet its food needs. This was ironic given the abundance of natural resources.

Pandit Deendayal analysed both the capitalist model and the socialist model and designed a third way—a way that enables the growth of every human while at the same time respecting the diversity and the integral nature of Bharat. With its focus on humanism and integral nature, the third way came to be known as integral humanism, or *Ekatma Manav Darshan*.

Let us now look at the economic principles of integral humanism.

Principles of Economic Policy

Any economic policy should be defined based on the following principles:

1. Equality and freedom in the economic life for every citizen.
2. Absence of exploitation in the economic transactions of the society.
3. Total employment (i.e. employment for all people).
4. Decentralization (decentralization results in democracy and economic freedom).
5. Use of natural resources in a balanced way (only use what you can replenish).
6. Appropriate use of technology.
7. Balanced economy with an optimum level of state interference in the economy.

We now take a look at some of the fundamental building blocks of a vibrant economy for Bharat.

Focus on Agriculture

A prosperous economy flows from a prosperous agriculture. Agriculture not only provides employment for a large majority of the population but also provides the means to feed a nation.

People working in the agriculture sector are the largest segment of customers for corporations making consumer goods. When the agriculture economy suffers, a big majority of the Indian population can no longer afford to purchase the consumer goods to meet their needs and wants. The quality of life of the farmer suffers. The corporations then focus on meeting the luxury needs of a small population. This creates a nation with a split personality. On one side, we have poverty with no life of dignity, and on the other side, we have pockets of the super rich. Development of agriculture is a prerequisite to the development of industries.

Development of agriculture means the availability of farm implements, seeds, fertilizers, and above all, water and electricity.

There is an emotional and cultural connection between a farmer and his land. Land provides a sense of pride and security. Hence, unlike in socialism, ownership of land is to be supported.

Limits may need to be imposed on how much land a single farmer can own, for the needs of an individual need to be balanced with those of the society. Ownership of land by tillers should be encouraged. With ownership, the farm worker would be motivated to optimize his farm yield for the short and the long-term.

Given the small size of land owned by any farmer, the use of tractors may not be viable. Also, livestock, such as bullocks, not only helps out in farming but also provides milk and dung. Cow dung is not only used as a fertilizer but also acts as a source of fuel. The emotional and cultural bonds that a farmer has with his livestock, which is evident in the various festivals, should not be severed. The use of fertilizers should be optimized so as to increase yield while at the same time not harming the long-term yield of the land.

Small-sized irrigation projects are needed in place of large dams. Large-scale irrigation creates waterlogging in soils, which results in salts surfacing on farmland. The land around large dams loses its natural quality of water percolation. This can cause floods even with less rainfall. Large dams also require huge amounts of capital and have longer gestation periods. Smaller irrigation projects not only require less capital but also provide employment to the rural population.

A minimum support price should be established for the farm produce. This ensures that there is not a big gap between the price of agricultural produce and the industrial consumer goods. Thus, the farmer has the purchasing power to buy the consumer goods to improve the quality of life, and the industrial corporations have a viable domestic market.

In addition to boosting agricultural production, an economic policy should also support equitable distribution for the farm produce.

A nation with rich natural resources, such as Bharat, must plan to be self-sufficient in foodgrains.

Industrial Focus

Bharat's industrial policy should have two objectives:

1. *Small industries around villages:* Economic policy should focus on the growth of small industries around villages

which produce consumer goods. As agriculture cannot provide employment all through the year, the growth of small industries will lead to total employment. Also, labour will not need to migrate to urban centres for work and will stay connected to their roots.

2. *Large-scale production:* Focus on the production of basic materials and capital. Given the long gestation periods and high capital needs for large-scale production plants, a state may support this sector.

The goal of any industrial policy is to produce goods that can be bought by the population to increase their standard of living. If an industrial policy only caters to the few rich, our nation will continue to remain in poverty.

Optimum Mix of Labour, Natural Resources, and Capital

Given the fact that Bharat is abundant in labour and natural resources but short on capital, any policy should optimize the mix as to:

1. Provide total employment.
2. Use natural resources only at the rate at which they can be replenished.
3. Efficient use of capital (government should optimize its own cost of administration so that the available capital can be deployed for growth of the economy).
4. Foreign capital, if used, should not come with any preconditions.

Decentralization

Decentralization means democracy and economic freedom. Planning should not begin in a centralized Planning Commission but should begin ground up from every village.

Promote the Defensive Power of the Nation

Economic policy should provide monetary support for building the defences of a nation. When the security of a nation and its people is at risk, there can be little development.

Restraint on Consumption

For a nation like Bharat, which is under foreign debt and has limited capital, restraints on consumption should be encouraged via education. Reducing the waste of national resources, such as water, electricity, and fuel, should be encouraged to support the economy.

To summarize, the goal of any economic policy should provide a life of dignity to every human by optimizing the mix of labour, capital, and natural resources.

A policy should optimize production, encourage restraints on consumption, and provide for equitable distribution.

Happiness of every human should be the mission of any *artha-neeti*, and the success of it can be measured by the principle of *antyodaya*—i.e. did the man at the lowest rung benefit?

□

6

Samaj-Shastra

Samaj-shastra is the study of society and how it relates to an individual and a nation. It is believed that society often yields more power than any state or government. Hence, it's important to study *samaj-shastra*.

The purpose of samaj-shastra is to bring about harmony between an individual and the society to ensure that there is no conflict between the two.

A society is an organized collection of individuals who have come together for a common purpose. A society is an organic entity. Like an individual, a society also has a body, mind, intellect, and soul. For example, when any club is formed, its members constitute the body; the activities of the club constitute its mind. The rules and regulations, its intellect, and the reason for the formation of the club are its soul.

A society has its own intellect, emotions, and strengths. An individual who is otherwise weak may end up doing a heroic deed for the society he belongs.

No individual can create everything that he needs on his own. To meet all his needs, any man needs the help of others—i.e. there is the principle of give and take. An individual can supply, at the most, a few needs of society, but what the society does for him is much greater.

The set of principles that maintains a balance between the individual and the society is called culture. It is via its culture that a society expresses itself. Culture creates this harmony and defines the code for individual and social behaviour. It is culture that brings about harmony between the interests of the society and the individual and ensures that there is no confrontation between the two.

The very first lessons that any human learns are in the family. Whenever there is an important event—be it happy or sad—the family comes together. A family is the fundamental building block of society. It is in the family that an individual first learns *samskars* (values). It is these *samskars* that will influence the behaviour and the relationship of an individual with society and the nation. For a healthy nation, one needs a healthy society, which is formed by healthy functional families. Dysfunctional families break the harmony and balance of a society, which weakens the nation in the long term.

In our culture, the term *family* is not limited to just the husband, wife, and kids. It extends to many other relationships, such as brothers, sisters, paternal and maternal uncles, grandfathers and grandmothers, sons-in-law and daughters-in-law, fathers-in-law and mothers-in-law, brothers-in-law and sisters-in-law, etc. A family has a sense of belonging and a shared life.

Family is an institution that provides support, meeting the most basic physical and emotional needs of every individual. A family is an institution where an individual first learns that he lives not only for himself, but he also has a sense of duty towards others. It is in the family that an individual first learns the value of service and sacrifice.

Every family has an unwritten but a well-understood code that decides on the needs and priorities of every member of the family. This code has a way to bring about an equitable distribution of resources among the members of the family. This comes about due to a shared sense of purpose, duty, and responsibility. What links to an individual to society is his family.

Just like a family, a society also has a shared sense of purpose, duties, and responsibilities. An individual and the society are connected by education, work, enjoyment, and sacrifice. It is the society which, via its various institutions, provides education and work. This helps an individual to meet his needs and wants.

In lieu, it is the duty of an individual to give back to society. This is termed as *sacrifice*.

If an individual uses society for his own gains but does not give back, the condition of the society and culture will deteriorate to an extent that it is unable to provide education and work to its citizens. It is in the interest of every individual that he strengthens the family system and the society. Just as the joys and sorrows of a family are shared, so must be the joys and the sorrows of society.

If after education a suitable job cannot be found or the job does not yield adequate income for meeting the needs of an individual, then the society has failed in its duty. Deendayal believes that the goals of an individual and society are complementary in nature and not contradictory.

Deendayal goes on to state that the individual and society should be mutually complementary and conducive to healthy mutual growth. Hence, there is a concept of a balanced society where the individual, while developing himself, fulfils the needs of the entire society and where the society, coordinating relations among the individuals itself, becomes strong, progressive, and elevated.

Deendayal says, 'In a social system, where the social behaviour of individuals promotes well-being, individual freedom and dignity will also be guaranteed.' Freedom of the individual, in this context, means that he is free to make himself capable of contributing to the progress of others. To play such a role, we ourselves must first become able and strong; he alone who has some power and strength of his own contribute. Being conducive does not mean being dependent on others. The desire to use individual capabilities for the maximum good of others will create opportunities for a continuous process of development.

The growth of an individual is linked to the growth of society. Great men are moulded not in isolation but by the culture and traditions of the society they come from. Individuals can only rise to realize their potentials when the society they live in provide the right conditioning environment.

In the history of Bharat, you will be find that when the nation was at its peak (e.g. the times of Maharana Kumbha in Rajasthan or the Vijayanagar dynasty down south), the society was strong, stable, and in harmony. Many a great men were born during those times that contributed back to society.

One of the most often asked question is 'How can I, as an individual, contribute to nation-building? The answer lies in paying your *social debt*. As long as we, as individuals, are contributing back to society, we are strengthening our society and our nation in return.

Hence, every individual should:

1. Give back to society with a sense of duty and responsibility.
2. Nurture and nourish the culture and our family system.

□

7
Rashtra-Neeti

The purpose of *rashtra-neeti* is to provide a roadmap to rebuild or develop a nation in tune with its ethos and traditions.

Rashtra-neeti is often misunderstood, as there is a lot of confusion between a nation and a state.

Rashtra (nation) and *rajya* (state) are not synonymous but represent different concepts. To understand *rashtra-neeti*, it is first important to understand the difference between the two.

Rajya, or a state, refers to a geographical or territorial entity that is inhabited by a community. *Rajya* can be formed or destroyed by political action. Any country establishes its identity by defining its territory, a flag, and an anthem.

In Bharat, we also have multiple states. The number of states is not fixed; new states get created from old ones. The territorial boundary of a state may also change from time to time.

Rajya also has a defined means for the administration of the state. The means of administration too change to enable the states to meet the needs. In an earlier time, we had monarchy, which gave way to a democratic form of government. *Rajya* is an organization created for the convenience of administration.

Nation, on the other hand, is a timeless entity. A nation is formed of people who live in a certain land, whose hearts are filled with pure love and dedication for the motherland, whose ideals about their friends and foes are the same, and who share a common set of heroes and leaders in history.

In addition to a territory and form of administration, a nation has:

1. A sense of purpose.
2. A shared view of history.
3. A binding force that glues it together in good and bad times.

To understand these concepts of a nation and a state, let us look at a few examples.

The state of Israel did not exist for 2,000 years. The Jews were distributed all across the world but had no territory to call their own. Even in exile, the Jewish society kept its sense of purpose alive—i.e. to create a homeland for all Jews. The Jewish society has a very strong sense of history. Their culture, way of life, and traditions kept them together even during the times leading up to the Second World War.

Thus, the nation of Israel was always alive even when there was no state.

On the other hand, we have Egypt. It was once a glorious civilization but is now confined to history books, museums, and Discovery Channel. The state of Egypt and the people who inhabit it are still very much there. But Egypt has lost its sense of purpose and the strong binding force that keeps it in tune with its traditional ethos. Hence, the old nation of Egypt is now lost forever.

Hence, there are two important pillars that sustain a nation—a sense of purpose and a strong binding glue that keeps it in tune with its ethos in good and bad times.

Pandit Deendayalji calls the first pillar (i.e. a sense of purpose) as *chiti* and the second pillar (i.e. strong binding glue) as *virat*.

Chiti represents our national spirit and character; it is the reason for our existence. *Chiti* also gives a sense of identity to a nation. For a nation called Bharat, what is our *chiti* and *virat*?

Since time immemorial, we have witnessed many wars and battles, struggles and revolutions. These wars, battles, struggles, and revolutions were always fought with one objective—to protect *dharma*.

Ram went to exile to follow his *dharma*; Sita went along to follow hers. We praise Ram for being a great son, but at the same time, we honour Prahlada, who killed his own father. We worship Krishna, who not only killed his own maternal uncle but also encouraged Arjuna to fight a war which meant killing one's own. We remember and revere Maharana Pratap, who died with the dream of freeing Chittor unfulfilled. Even an animal such as Chetak, the horse, is revered for following his own *dharma*.

We worship and revere those who have always fought for protecting *dharma*. This worship comes naturally to us; we need not be told or trained.

When there is *adharma*, society will rise, and leaders will emerge to bring back *dharma*, a force that sustains and restores harmony.

The *chiti*, or the purpose of Bharat, is to protect *dharma*. *Dharma* here is not a religion or a mode of worship but the force that sustains and stabilizes life. Whenever *dharma* gets protected, the *chiti* gets stronger and so does the nation called Bharat.

The decline and slavery of Bharat began the day when we neglected our sense of purpose and did not protect *dharma*. Once the *chiti* of the nation weakens, its decline becomes inevitable.

The decline of Bharat also began with the weakening of its *chiti*. Reconstruction of a nation also begins the rekindling of its *chiti*.

Great reformers, such as Adi Shankaracharya, Swami Vivekananda, Aurobindo Ghose, Mahatma Gandhi, and many others, who helped rebuild Bharat began by reigniting or strengthening our chiti. If Bharat needs to be rebuilt to regain its true potential, it can only be built on the spiritual platform called dharma.

As the old saying goes, 'धर्मो रक्षति रक्षितः (i.e. *dharma* only protects those which protect *dharma*).

The life of a nation is not made or destroyed in one day or a few years, as the strengthening or weakening of the *chiti* takes years and generations.

It is important to frame policies that maintain a sense of harmony between individuals and other individuals, between individuals and society, between different communities in a society, and between our needs of consumption and the resources provided by nature. This means of strengthening our *chiti* is called *rashtra-neeti*.

Rashtra-neeti involves strengthening *dharma*, our ethos, and our way of life so as to nurture and nourish our nation for generations to come.

Chiti, the soul of a nation, is accompanied by another force called *virat*. According to Deendayalji, the organized and unified fighting strength which protects the nation from aggression and dissension is called virat.

Virat is the *Shakti* generated by the organized strength of society that can help fight the gravest of aggressions. For Bharat, our *virat* lies in our culture.

For thousands of years, forces have invaded Bharat from across the globe. The invading armies had superior weapons and forces; they had no moral scruples in dealing with the population. They killed, raped, looted with ease, and erased temples to demean and demoralize the population. Life was without dignity.

Despite the most barbaric of means used, the nation fought back. Many nations across the world ceased to exist, but Bharat fought back.

How did Bharat fight back? First, by rekindling our *chiti* (i.e. *dharma*) and fighting back with our *virat* (i.e. culture). Despite destroying institutions such as temples, our virat (i.e. our culture) continued to live in every home. The moment our *chiti* was awakened, our *virat* took over, and we fought back.

Bharat as a nation has not only survived and grown for tens of thousands of years on the two pillars of *chiti* and *virat*. Time and again, we have leaders or reformers have who come to strengthen *dharma* (our *chiti*), which in turn has strengthened our culture (our *virat*).

An organized society with an awakened *chiti* will always fight back against a state or a government which is not functioning properly (i.e. functioning contrary to our *chiti*). When a bad government is tolerated, it is an indication of a society devoid of *chiti*. When chiti is weak, even having a *virat* is not of much help. The degeneration of the nation sets in. Destruction of a nation begins with the weakening of *chiti*.

The decline of Bharat had in the past begun with the weakening of *dharma* and the contamination of our culture. Reconstruction of Bharat will too commence when the process to awaken our *dharma* and strengthening of culture begins.

Thus, unlike other countries where nationalism is based on territory, race, or language, in Bharat our common culture is the foundation of our nationalism. The nation of Bharat in this sense is not limited to the political boundaries of India but extends to regions, which share a common culture. Nationalism based on culture unities, whereas (as seen in the world wars), nationalism based on race, language, or territory leads to conflict and chaos.

Having discussed at length on *rashtra* (nation), let's turn our attention to *rajya* (state).

As discussed, *rajya*, or a state, is a means of administration designed to achieve the goals of a nation. A state exists to serve the nation and provide the ways and means for the nation to meet its goals—both short term and long term.

There are a few duties which every state needs to perform:

1. *Law and order:* The first and the fundamental duty of any form of administration is to maintain an atmosphere of peace and order to make the life of its people secure and growth-oriented. A state must act swiftly against anti-national and anti-social forces. A state has to ensure that the law prevails at all times.
2. *Solve day-to-day problems:* The second duty of the state is to solve problems that impact the day-to-day life of every citizen. It is the responsibility of the state to define policies and programmes that address basic day-to-day issues. In addition to serving the needs of the nation, a state has to serve every citizen to improve the quality of life of every individual.
3. *Foreign policy:* A state has to develop respectable relationships with other nations to further its own interest.
4. *Protect the nation:* The most important duty of any state is to protect the nation.

Per Deendayalji, a state exists for a nation. A nation is not born for politics. A political government must do everything to enhance the national interest. Politics which weakens a nation is considered despicable.

When a state fails to perform its duties, the nation acts in accordance with its *chiti* and *virat*. Society comes together to change the government. At times, the nation decides to change the state for good as seen in revolutions across the world.

Rashtra-neeti comes first, and the objective of *raj-neeti* and *artha-neeti* is to support nation-building.

Many problems that are present in Bharat and the world are caused by the failure to understand the concept of a nation. A state is assumed to be a nation, and *raj-neeti* is confused for *rashtra-neeti*.

It is important for every citizen to understand the concepts of the nation. *Rashtra-neeti* helps us differentiate between what is good for the nation and what is not. It's the only parameter to judge national interest. When the nation perishes, so does state, society, and every individual.

Rashtra-neeti is the only way to secure for freedom—political, economic, and social. It is the duty of every citizen to protect our *rashtra*.

□

8
Vision for India

At the fourteenth annual session of the Jan Sangh, Pandit Deendayal Upadhyaya was elected as its twelfth president. Since the inception of the Jan Sangh, Deendayal had been its guiding light.

He not only defined the ideology and policies of the Jan Sangh but also built an organization of cadres committed to the ideology and the principles of the Jan Sangh. Deendayal went to define how the party should conduct its *raj-neeti* and define its *artha-neeti* and *rashtra-neeti*.

Having built a party and defined its policies, the time had arrived to provide a vision for India. This he did in his presidential address in Calicut in December 1967.

Any vision has to be in tune with the cultural ethos and traditions of a nation. Like any vision, a vision for a civilization such as Bharat, which is thousands of years old, should be inspiring yet based on *dharma*. A vision should learn from the past but seek to build a future.

In his presidential speech, Deendayal paints a very clear picture of what a rebuilt Bharat would look like.

While we do draw inspiration from the past, we do not regard the past as the highest pinnacle of our achievement; while we have a realistic approach to the present, we do not feel tied down even to the present; and while we do have before our eyes a vision of a great future for this country, we are not mere visionaries but are *karmayogis* resolved to translate our vision into reality.

We are pledged to the service not of any particular community or section but of the entire nation. Every countryman is blood of our blood and flesh of our flesh. We shall not rest till we are able to give to every one of them a sense of pride that they are children of *Bharatmata*.

We shall make Mother India *sujala suphala* (laden with fruits and overflowing with water) in the real sense of these words. As *Dashapraharana Dharini Durga* (Goddess Durga with her ten weapons) she would be able to vanquish evil; as Lakshmi she would be able to disburse prosperity all over and as Saraswati she would dispel the gloom of ignorance and spread the radiance of knowledge all around her. With faith in ultimate victory, let us dedicate ourselves to this task.

Pandit Deendayal's idea of India is:

1. A nation which has Shakti of its own to protect itself and its citizens.
2. A nation with bountiful agricultural produce to feed itself.
3. A nation which takes from nature only what it can replenish.
4. A nation with enough wealth which is distributed equitably.
5. A nation with knowledge to bring all-around development for itself and the world.

Bharat will be rebuilt when Deendayal's idea of India is realized. This was the first time since the independence of Bharat that a mainstream political party presented before the nation a vision that would guide its politics and policies. For the first time since independence, Bharat has set a goal for itself.

□

9

Ekatma Manav Darshan: Vision for the World

Despite being in existence for thousands of years, the world today stands at the crossroads. Despite the advances of science and various models of development, a big part of the world lives in poverty. Those with access to wealth yearn for peace within. Today there are conflicts among humans in every part of the world. There is a greater conflict between humans and nature.

Pandit Deendayalji has put forward a model of development which is not only applicable to India but to the world at large. This model is called *Ekatma Manav Darshan*, or integral humanism.

The foundational feature of *Ekatma Manav Darshan* is that it looks upon life as a whole—i.e. it puts forward an integrated viewpoint.

Individual, family, society, nation, humanity, and the universe are integral in nature. They are so interconnected and complementary to one another that the development of one cannot be at the cost of others.

The first component of the integrated whole is *vyasthi*, or an individual. An individual can develop when the family system develops. A family can develop when the society develops. An individual has a sense of duty towards the society. This is a bidirectional relationship wherein both the individual and the society mutually develop each other. When an individual takes on the role of a parasite, the society suffers, and soon the individual will suffer too.

Education and work flow from society to individuals. When the individual shares the fruits of work back with society, both flourish.

Any individual's goal in life is to satisfy two conditions:

1. Individual must meet his or her own needs or wants in line with *dharma*.
2. Progress of an individual must be complementary to the progress of society.

The theory of *Ekatma Manav Darshan* calls for every individual to meet his or her own needs and wants in line with *dharma* but, at the same time, do so with restraint and spirit of sacrifice for the co-development of society. An individual's progress must never stand in the way of social progress. This is known as *vyasthi dharma*.

As a member of the world community, we must discharge our responsibilities. If we possess something that may prove helpful to world progress, we should not hesitate in imparting it to the world.

Society, in turn, must ensure that an individual has access to education and is able to find employment to meet his or her needs and wants. The complementary, cooperative, and connected relationship between an individual, family, and society is called *samasthi*. *Samasthi dharma* sustains both an individual and society and is a prerequisite for the development of the nation. *Samasthi dharma* also ensures that members of the society who are unable to meet their own needs are taken care of by the society.

This integrated viewpoint is not limited to individuals, family, society, and nation but extends to all of humanity. For peace and prosperity, nations should not only look after their own interest. There is a sense duty that each nation has towards other nations and the world at large.

This integrated viewpoint which sees the world as one is critical to address many of the global problems we face today. It's only when we see the entire humanity as one that we will discharge our duties towards our fellow citizens of the world.

What should drive all our global aid programmes is not diplomacy or geopolitical give and take but our belief that the world is one big family. When any nation fails to meet its global obligations, the world suffers.

This 'humanity is one principle', which calls for global cooperation and collaboration, is called *shristhi*.

The last piece of the integrated whole is called *parameshthi*, or the universe. Humanity is dependent on nature for its survival. When the reserves of nature perish, so will humanity. Hence, natural resources should be consumed with a sense of trusteeship. As guardians of natural resources, let us take from nature only what we need and what can naturally be replenished. This is referred to as *parameshthi dharma*.

Through his work on integral humanism, Pandit Deendayalji has presented a vision for the world—a vision which claims that the world is one, or 'वसुधैव कुटुम्बकम्'. The various parts of the world—the individuals, societies, and nations—are interconnected to one another with bonds of duty and sacrifice. When these bonds of duty and sacrifice for the greater good are strengthened, humanity will emerge stronger.

Pandit Deendayal's vision for the world is in tune with Bharat's cultural ethos and can be summarized as:

सर्वे भवन्तु सुखिन= सर्वे सन्तु निरामया।
सर्वे भद्राणि पश्यन्तु मा कश्चित् दु:खभाग् भवेत्।
ॐ शान्ति: शान्ति: शान्ति: ॥

□

10

Tyag, *Tapasya*, *Seva*, and *Balidaan*

The life of any *rishi* can be summed up in four words: *tyag*, *tapasya*, *seva*, and *balidaan*. Pandit Deendayal Upadhyaya was a *rishi* in a true sense. He was a bright young scholar who gave up his family and career to serve society. This *tyag* was followed by decades of *tapasya*, which resulted in building a political alternative and a development model in line with Bharat's cultural ethos. The *tapasya* showed results with non-Congress government in many states across India in the 1960s.

Deendayal dedicated his life to the service of motherland. His *seva* resulted in his providing a vision for Bharat and a roadmap of how to achieve it.

Within weeks of taking charge as the president of the Jan Sangh and articulating his vision and roadmap for India, Deendayal was assassinated on 11 February 1968 while travelling in a train at Mughalsarai. No one was arrested, and the murder remains a mystery. Bharat had once again lost a great son; for the second time, the Jan Sangh had lost its leader.

Panditji's *balidaan* was not in vain. His ideas, ideology, and principles continue to live in *karyakartas* till today.

As Bharat begins its reconstruction today, we can better be prepared, thanks to the *tyag*, *tapasya*, *seva*, and *balidaan* of one our great *rishis*, Pandit Deendayal Upadhyaya.

□

11
Integral Humanism

Even after 17 years of independence we have still to decide what direction we should adopt to realise our cherished dream of all-round development in the lives of our countrymen. Normally, people are not prepared to seriously consider this question. They think only of the problems which they face from time to time. Sometimes economic problems are viewed with concern and an attempt is made to resolve them, and at other times, social or political problems come to the forefront claiming attention. Not knowing fundamentally the direction in which we all are to go, these efforts are not accompanied by sufficient enthusiasm, nor do they give a feeling of satisfaction to the people engaged in these efforts. These efforts produce only a fraction of the results that they ought to have produced.

Modern versus Ancient

However, there are two distinct types of people who do suggest some definite direction. There are some who suggest that we must go back to the position when we lost our independence and restart from there. On the other hand, there are people who would like to discard all that has originated here in Bharat and they are not ready to give a second thought to it. They seem to think that Western life and thoughts are the last word in progress and all of them should be imported here if we are to develop. Both these lines of thought are incorrect, though they do represent partial truths and it will not be proper to reject them altogether.

They, who advocate starting from where we left off a thousand years ago, forget that whether it may or may not be desirable, it is definitely impossible because wheels of time cannot be turned back.

Old cannot be Negated

Whatever we have done during the last one thousand years, whether it was thrust upon us or we acquired it with great efforts, we cannot go along by discarding all that now. Besides, we too have original creations in the life of our society. We did not always remain mere passive witness to whatever new challenging situations arose, nor did we merely react to every alien action. We too, have attempted to reshape our life as was required to face the new situations. Therefore, we cannot afford to shut our eyes to all that has happened in the past one thousand years.

Foreign Ideas are not Universal

Similarly, those who would like to make Western ideologies the basis of our progress, forget that these ideologies have arisen in certain special situations and times. They are not necessarily universal. They cannot be free from the limitations of the particular people and their culture which gave birth to these *isms*. Besides, many of these are already out of date. The principles of Marx have changed both with the changing times as well as with varying conditions, to the extent that parrot-like repetition of Marxism for solving the problems facing our country, would amount to a reactionary attitude rather than a scientific and pragmatic one. It is indeed surprising, that they who claim to reform the society by removing dead traditions, themselves fall prey to some outdated foreign traditions.

Learn, But Do Not Ape Others

Every country has its own peculiar historical, social and economic situation, and its leaders decide the remedies for the ills that beset the country from time to time, taking into consideration its background. It is illogical to believe that remedies which the leaders of one country decide to try for their problems are likely to be effective as such to all other peoples.

A simple illustration will suffice. Even though the basic organic activity is the same in all human beings, the drugs which may be helpful in England may not prove equally helpful in Bharat. Diseases also depend upon climate, water, dietary habits and heredity. Even though the external symptoms may be apparently similar, the same drug does not necessarily cure all persons. Those who apply a single panacea to all diseases must be considered quacks rather than doctors. Therefore, Ayurveda states "यद्देशस्य तो जन्तुः तद्देशस्य तस्योषधम्" i.e. for the disease in each place a remedy suitable to that place is found. Therefore, it is neither possible nor wise to adopt foreign isms in our country in the original form in toto. It will not be helpful in achieving happiness and prosperity.'

On the other hand, it needs to be realised that not all the thoughts and principles that have sprung up elsewhere are necessarily local in space and time. The response of human beings in a particular place, time and social atmosphere may, and does, in many cases, have relation and use to other human beings elsewhere and at other times. Therefore, to ignore altogether the development in other societies, past or present, is certainly unwise. Whatever truths these developments contain must be taken note of and accepted. The rest must be scrupulously avoided. While absorbing the wisdom of other societies, it is only proper that we avoid their mistakes or perversities. Even their wisdom should be adapted to our particular circumstances. In brief, we must absorb the knowledge and gains of the entire humanity so far as eternal principles and truths are concerned. Of these, the ones that originated in our midst have to be clarified and adapted to changed times, and those that we take from other societies have to be adapted to our conditions.

Conflicting Ideals

Western political thought has accepted Nationalism, Democracy, and Socialism or Equality, as ideals. Besides, now and then, there have been attempts directed at world unity which took the shape of the League of Nations, and after the Second World War, the United Nations Organisation. For a variety of reasons these have not succeeded. However, these definitely were attempts in that direction. All these ideals have in practice proved to be incomplete and mutually opposing.

Nationalism led to conflict between nations which led in turn to global conflict. Whereas if *status quo* is regarded as synonymous with world peace, the aspirations of many small nations to be independent would remain ever unfulfilled. World unity and nationalism conflict with each other. Some advocate suppression of nationalism for world unity, whereas others regard world unity as a utopian ideal and emphasise national interest to the utmost.

Similar difficulty arises in reconciling socialism and democracy. Democracy grants individual liberty, but the same is used by the capitalist system for exploitation and monopolisation. Socialism was brought in to end exploitation, but it destroyed freedom and dignity of the individual.

Mankind stands confused and is unable to decide what the correct path is for future progress. The West is not in a position to say with confidence that, "This alone and no other", is the right path. It is itself groping. Therefore, simply to follow the West would be an instance of the blind being led by the blind.

Culture should be a Consideration

In this situation, our attention is claimed by the *Bharatiya* culture. Is it possible that our culture can point the direction to the world?

From the national standpoint we shall have to consider our culture, because that is our very nature. Independence is intimately related to one's own culture. If culture does not form the basis of independence, then the political movement for self rule would be reduced simply to a scramble by selfish and power-seeking persons. Self rule can be meaningful only if it becomes an instrument for the expression of our culture. Such expression will not only contribute to our progress, but the effort required will also give us the experience of joy. Therefore, both from the national as well as human standpoint, it has become essential that we think of the principles of *Bharatiya* culture. If with its help, we can reconcile the various ideals of Western political thought, then it will be an icing on the cake (मणि-कांचन सयोग). These

Western principles are a product of revolution in human thought and social conflict. They represent one or the other aspiration of mankind and it is not proper to ignore them.

Bharatiya Culture is Holistic

The first characteristic of *Bharatiya* culture is that it looks upon life as an integrated whole. It has an integrated viewpoint. To think of parts may be proper for a specialist, but it is not useful from the practical standpoint. The confusion in the West arises primarily from its tendency to think of life in parts and then to attempt to put them together by patchwork.

We do admit that there is diversity and plurality in life, but we have always attempted to discover the unity behind them. This attempt is thoroughly scientific. The scientists always attempts to discover order in the apparent disorder in the universe, to find out the principles governing the universe and frame practical rules on the basis of these principles. Chemists discovered that a few elements comprise the entire physical world. Physicists went one step further and showed that even these elements pulsate with energy. Today we know, that the entire universe is only a form of energy.

Philosophers are also basically scientists. The Western philosophers reached up to the principle of duality. Hegel put forward the principle of thesis, anti-thesis and synthesis. Karl Marx used his principle as a basis and presented his analysis of history and economics.

Darwin considered the principle of survival of the fittest as the sole basis of life. But we, in this country, perceived the basic unity of all life. Even the dualists have believed nature and spirit to be complementary to each other rather than contradictory. The diversity in life is merely an expression of the internal unity. There is complementarity underlying the diversity. The unity in seed finds expression in various forms—the roots, the trunk, the branches, the leaves, the flowers and the fruits of the tree. All these have different forms and colours and even to some extent different properties. Still we recognise their relation of unity with each other through the seed.

Conflict – Sign of Cultural Regression

Unity in diversity and the expression of unity in various forms have remained the central thought of *Bharatiya* culture. If this truth is whole-heartedly accepted, then there will not exist any cause for conflict among various powers. Conflict is not a sign of culture or nature; rather it is a symptom of perversion. The law of the jungle – 'Survival of the Fittest'—which the West discovered in recent years was known to our philosophers. We have recognised desire, anger, etc, among the six lower tendencies of human nature, but we did not use them as the foundation or the basis of civilised life or culture. There are thieves and robbers in society. It is essential to save ourselves and society from these elements. We cannot consider them as our ideals or standards of human behaviour. Survival of the fittest is the law of the jungle. Civilisations have developed not on the basis of this law, but by consideration of how the operation of this law could be reduced to the minimum in human life. If we wish to progress, we have to keep this history of civilisation before our minds.

Mutual Cooperation

Cooperation also obtains in abundance just as conflict and competition in this world. Vegetation and animal life keep each other alive. We get our oxygen supply with the help of vegetation, whereas we provide carbon dioxide, so essential for the growth of vegetable life. This mutual cooperation sustains life on this earth.

The recognition of this element of mutual sustenance among different forms of life and taking that as the basis of an effort to make human life mutually sustaining is the prime characteristic of civilisation. To mould nature (प्रकृति) to achieve social goals is culture (संस्कृति), but when this nature leads to social conflict, it is perversion (विकृति). Culture does not disregard or deny nature. Rather it enhances those elements in nature which are helpful in sustaining life in this universe, makes it fuller and richer, and curbs others which obstruct or destroy life.

Let us take a simple illustration. The relationships such as brother and sister, mother and son, father and son, are natural. These are same both in man as well as among animals. Just as two brothers are sons of one mother so also two calves have a single mother cow. Where then lies the difference? The animals forget these natural relationships. They cannot build up an edifice of civilisation on these relations. But men use this natural relation as a basis to construct a more harmonious order in life, to establish other relationships flowing from these basic relationships, so as to knit the whole society as a single unit of cooperation. Thus various values and traditions are built. Standards of good and bad are determined accordingly. In society, we find instances of both affection as well as enmity between brothers. But we consider affection good, and aim at enhancing affectionate brotherly relations. The opposite tendency is disapproved. If conflict and enmity are made the basis of human relationships, and if on this basis history is analysed, then it would be futile to dream of world peace resulting out of such a course of action.

A mother brings up her children. A mother's love is considered as the highest love. On such a basis alone, we can devise the rules regulating the life of mankind. Sometimes there are examples of selfishness and cruelty of a mother towards her child. Among some species of animals, the mother devours her progeny to satisfy her hunger. On the other hand, among monkeys, the mother carries her child long after its death. Both types of behaviour are found among living beings. Which of these two principles of nature can be made the basis of a civilised life? We cannot but conclude that, that alone which helps to sustain life can be chosen, the contrary cannot lead to a civilised life. Human nature has both tendencies, anger and greed on the one hand, and love and sacrifice on the other. All these are present in our nature. Anger, greed, etc. are natural to man and beasts alike. For this reason, if we make anger a basis of our life and arrange our efforts accordingly, then the result will be a lack of harmony in our life. Therefore the exhortation, "Do not yield to anger". Even when anger arises in one's mind, one can exercise control over it and one should do so. Thus control becomes a standard of our life and not anger.

Such laws are known as the principles of ethics. These principles are not framed by anyone. They are discovered. A suitable analogy is that of the law of gravitation. If we throw a stone, it falls on the ground. This law of gravitation was not framed by Newton. He discovered it. When he saw an apple falling on the ground from the branch, he realised there must exist such a law. Thus he discovered this law, he did not frame it. Similarly, there are certain principles of human relations. For instance, if one feels anger, one must keep it under control. Such an act will be beneficial to all. These principles of ethics are, therefore, discovered. "Do not tell a lie to one another; say what you know to be true". This is a principle. Its usefulness becomes apparent at every step in life. We appreciate a truthful person. If we tell a lie, we ourselves feel unhappy: life cannot go on, there will be great confusion.

A child does not speak untruths by nature. Often, parents teach their child to speak untruths. When the child desires something which the parents do not wish to give him, they conceal the object and tell the child that the desired object has disappeared. The child may be fooled a couple of times, but soon he knows the real situation and learns to speak untruths. The fact that, by nature a person is truthful, is a law that is discovered. Many other principles of ethics are similarly discovered. They are not arbitrarily framed by someone. In Bharat, these principles are termed *Dharma* – the laws of life. All those principles which bring about harmony, peace and progress in the life of mankind are included in this term *Dharma*. On the sound basis of *Dharma* then, we must proceed with the analysis of life as an integral whole.

When nature is channelised according to the principles of *Dharma*, we have culture and civilisation. It is indeed this culture which will enable us to sustain and sublimate the life of mankind. *Dharma* is translated here as law. The English word 'religion' is not the correct translation for '*Dharma*'. As pointed out earlier, an integrated life is not only the foundation and the underlying principle of culture, but also its aims and ideals.

Happiness of an Individual

We have thought of life as integrated not only in the case of collective or social life but also in the individual life. Normally, an individual is thought of in the physical bodily form. Physical comfort and luxury are considered happiness. But we know that mental worry destroys bodily happiness. Everyone desires physical comfort. But if a person is imprisoned, and there he is given the finest of foods, will he be happy? A person does not experience joy on getting nice food if this is also accompanied by a few abuses.

There is a well-known incident in the Mahabharata. When Lord Krishna went to Hastinapura as an emissary of the Pandavas, Duryodhana invited him to enjoy his hospitality. Lord Krishna declined his invitation and went instead to Vidura's home. Overjoyed by the visit of this much-revered guest, Vidura's wife served the banana skins while throwing away the kernel. But Lord Krishna enjoyed even the meal of banana skin. That is why it is said, "Even a modest meal served with dignity and affection, tastes better than the best delicacies served with disrespect". It is necessary, therefore, to take note of mental happiness as well.

Similarly, there is an intellectual happiness which must also be considered. Even after a person gets comforts for the body and prominence, affection, etc., which please the mind, but if he is involved in some intellectual confusion, he is reduced to a state almost similar to madness. And what is madness itself? A lunatic may have all physical comforts, he may be perfectly healthy and properly cared for by his relatives, but he does not possess intellectual happiness. Intellectual peace is also essential and important. We will have to take all these things into consideration.

Political Ambition and its Realisation by Human Beings

Body, mind, intellect and the soul—these four make up an individual. But these are integrated. We cannot think of each part separately. The confusion that has arisen in the West is due to the fact that they have treated each of the above aspects of a human being separately and without any relation to the rest. When there was movement for a democratic structure, they proclaimed, "Man is a political animal", and therefore his political aspirations must be attended to. Why should only one person be the king and all others his subjects? Let everyone rule. In order to satisfy this political man, they gave him the right to vote. Now he did get the right to vote, but at the same time other rights diminished. Then the question arose, "The voting right is nice, but what about food? What if there is nothing to eat?" They wondered. "Now that you have the voting right, you are the king. Why need you worry?" But man replied, " What shall I do with the State if I don't get any food? I have no use of this voting right. I want bread first." Then came Karl Marx and said, "Yes, bread is the most important thing. The State belongs to the 'haves'. So let us fight for bread." He saw man as primarily made up of body, wanting bread. But those who followed the path shown by Karl Marx came to realise that they had neither bread nor voting rights. At the opposite end, there is the U.S.A. There is both bread as well as voting rights. Even then there is lack of peace and happiness. The U.S.A. tops the list in number of suicides, number of mental patients and number of persons using tranquillisers to get sleep. People are puzzled as to the cause of this new situation. Man obtained bread, he got his voting right, still there is no peace, no happiness.

Now they want back their peaceful sleep. Sound and undisturbed sleep is a scarce commodity in present day America. The thinkers are coming to realise that there lies somewhere, a fundamental lacuna in their system of life due to which they are not happy, even after they have attained so much prosperity and affluence.

Bharatiya Approach to Life

The reason is that they have not thought of the integrated human being. In our country, we have thoroughly considered this matter. That is why we have stated that progress of man means simultaneous progress of the body, mind, intellect and soul of man. Often it has been propagated that *Bharatiya* culture thinks of salvation of the soul, that it does not bother about the rest.

This is wrong. We do think of the soul, but it is not true that we do not consider body, mind and intellect of much importance. Others gave importance to the body alone. Therefore, our attention to the soul appears unique. With the passage of time, this created an impression that we are concerned only with the soul and not with other aspects of the human being.

A young, unmarried boy cares for his mother, but after marriage he cares both for his wife as well as his mother, and discharges his responsibilities towards both of them. Now if anyone says that this man has no love for his mother, it would be untrue. A wife loves only her husband at first, but after the birth of a child, she loves both her husband and child. Sometimes an unthoughtful husband feels that his wife neglects him after the birth of their child. But this is generally not correct. If that were true then the wife has certainly not performed her duty.

Our Needs—Four Purusharthas

Similarly, while we recognise the need to pay attention to the soul, we do not neglect the body. *Upanishads* declare in unambiguous words नाऽयमात्मा बलहीनेन, लभ्यः *i.e.* a weakling cannot realise the Self. Again शरीरमाद्यं खलु धर्मसाधनम् *i.e.* the body is truly the primary instrument to discharge the responsibilities that *Dharma* enjoins. The fundamental difference between our position and that of the West is that, whereas they have regarded the body and the satisfaction of its desires as the aim, we regard the body as an instrument for achieving our aims. We have recognised the importance of the body only in this light. The satisfaction of our bodily needs is necessary, but we don't consider this to be the sole aim of all our efforts. Here in Bharat, we have placed before ourselves the ideal of the four-fold responsibilities of catering to the needs of body, mind, intellect and soul with a view to achieve the integrated progress of man. *Dharma*, *Artha*, *'Kama'* and *Moksha* are the four kinds of *Purusharthas* (पुरुषार्थ) – human effort. *Purushartha* means effort which befit a man. The longings for *Dharma*, *Artha*, *Kama* and *Moksha* are inborn in man, and the satisfaction of these gives him joy (आनंद). Of these four efforts too, we have thought in an integrated way. Even though *Moksha* has been considered the highest of these *Purusharthas*, efforts for *Moksha* alone are not considered to bring benefit to the soul. On the other hand, a person who engages in action, while remaining unattached to its fruits, is said to achieve *Moksha* inevitably and earlier.

Artha (अर्थ) includes what are known as political and economic policies. According to the ancients, it used to include Justice and Punishment as well as Economics (दंडनीति और वार्त्ता). *Kama* relates to the satisfaction of various natural desires.

Dharma includes all those rules, fundamental principles and ethical codes in accordance with which all the activities in respect of *Artha* and *Kama* are to be carried out, and all the goals thereof to be achieved. This alone will ensure progress in an integrated and harmonious manner, and lead ultimately to *Moksha.*

Importance of *Dharma*

Thus, even though *Dharma* regulates *Artha* and *Kama*, all the three are interrelated and mutually complementary. *Dharma* helps achieve *Artha.* Even in business one requires honesty, restraint, truthfulness, etc., which are the attributes of *Dharma.* Without these qualities one cannot earn money. It must be admitted that *Dharma* is instrumental in attaining *Artha* and *Kama.* Americans proclaimed, "Honesty is the best business policy". In Europe, they said, "Honesty is the best policy". We go one step forward and assert "Honesty is not a policy but a principle", i.e. we believe in *Dharma* not just because it is instrumental in acquiring *Artha,* but because it is a fundamental principle of civilised life. *Karma* too can be attained only through *Dharma.* Having produced the material things, such as nice food, when, where, how, and in what measure it will be used, can be determined only by *Dharma.* If a sick person eats food meant for a healthy one and *vice versa,* both of them will be at a disadvantage. *Dharma* helps in restraining the natural tendencies of man, whereby he is able to determine what is beneficial to him, apart from what is pleasurable. Hence *Dharma* is given the foremost place in our culture.

Dharma is of primary importance, but we should not forget that it is not possible to practise *Dharma* in the absence of *Artha.* There is a saying, "What sin will not be committed by one who is starving? Those who have lost everything become ruthless". Driven by hunger, even a rishi like Vishwamitra broke into the house of a hunter and ate the flesh of a dog. Therefore, we are enjoined to see that there is enough wealth created continuously, since wealth also strengthens *Dharma.*

Similarly, the government has to maintain law and order and prevent chaos which definitely destroys *Dharma.* At the time of chaos, the law of the jungle prevails where the strong feed upon the weak. Therefore, stability of the State is also essential for the prevalence of *Dharma*.

Dispensation of Justice

Artha is inclusive of political aspects of life as well. Excessive power of the State is also harmful for *Dharma*. It was said that a king should be neither too harsh nor too soft with his people. Excessive reliance on harsh measures produces a feeling of revolt in people. When the State usurps the rightful place of *Dharma*, then there is this evil of the preponderance of power of the State. *Dharma* suffers thereby. This is the reason for the decline of *Dharma* in ruthless States.

When the State acquires all powers, political and economic, the result is a decline of *Dharma*. In this way, if the State has unlimited powers, the whole society looks towards the State for everything. Officers of the Government neglect their duties and develop vested interests. These are all signs of the preponderance of powers of the State, whereby *Dharma* suffers a setback. Hence *Artha* should not be allowed to acquire a hold in either of these two ways.

Kama too has been considered on the same lines. If the physical needs are neglected, and desires entirely suppressed, *Dharma* does not grow. *Dharma* cannot be observed if one has no food to eat. If the fine arts, which satisfy the mind, are altogether stopped, then the civilising influence on people will not be present. The mind will become perverse and *Dharma* neglected. On the other hand, if greediness of the gluttons of Rome or sensuousness of Yayati prevails, then duties will be forgotten. Hence *Kama* too must be pursued in consonance with *Dharma*.

We have thus considered the life of an individual in a thorough and integrated manner. We have set the aim of developing body, mind, intellect as well as soul in a balanced way. We have tried to satisfy the manifold aspirations of man, taking care that efforts to satisfy two different aspirations are not mutually conflicting. This is the integrated picture of the four-fold aspirations for an individual. This concept of a complete human being, an integrated individual, is both our goal as well as our path. What should be the relation of this integrated human being with the society and how the interests of the society should be promoted will be discussed tomorrow.

23rd April, 1965

□

Harmony between the Individual, and the Supreme Collectivity

Yesterday we considered man as an individual. There are different aspects to an individual's personality, different levels of needs for an individual in order to develop a complete personality. To satisfy the needs progressively but simultaneously at all levels, certain specific kinds of efforts (पुरुषार्थ) are needed. These, too, were considered. Man does not exist merely as an individual. The individual comprising body, mind, intellect and soul is not limited to a singular 'I' but is also inseparably related to the plural 'We'. Therefore we must also think of the group or the society.

Theories About the formation of Society

It is a simple truth that society is a group of men. But how did society come into being? Many views have been put forward by philosophers. Those propounded in the West and on which the Western socio-political structure is based can be broadly summarised as "society is a group of individuals who, having entered into an agreement among themselves, brought it into being". This view is known as the 'Social Contract Theory'. Individual is given greater importance in this view.

If there are any differences in different Western views, these pertain only to the questions, namely, "If the individual produced a society, then, in whom does the residual power remain vested – in the society or the individual? Does the individual have the right to change the society? Can the society impose a variety of regulations on the individual and claim a right to the allegiance of the individual to itself? Or is the individual free in regard to these questions?"

समाज स्वयंभू है Society is Self Existent

There is a controversy in the West on this question. Some have advocated the supremacy of the society and from this a conflict has arisen. The view that individuals have brought the society into being is fundamentally incorrect. It is true that society is composed of a number of individuals. Yet it is not created by the individuals, nor does it come into being by the mere coming together of a number of individuals. In our view, society is self-born. Like an individual, society comes into existence in an organic way. People do not produce society. It is not a sort of club, or some joint-stock company, or a registered cooperative society. In reality, society is an entity with its own "SELF", its own life; it is a sovereign being like an individual; it is an organic entity. We have not accepted the view that society is some arbitrary association. It has its own life. Society too has its body, mind, intellect and soul. Some Western psychologists are beginning to accept this truth. McDougal has propounded a new branch of psychology called "group mind". He has accepted that the group has its own mind, its own psychology, its own methods of thinking and action.

A group has its feelings too. These are not exactly similar to the individual's feelings. Group feelings cannot be considered a mere arithmetical addition of individual feeling. Group strength too is not a mere sum of individual strength. The intellect, emotions, energies and strength of a group are fundamentally different from those of an individual. Therefore, at times it is experienced that even a weakling, despite his individual weak physique, turns out to be a heroic member of society. Sometimes an individual may be ready to put up with an affront to his personal self, but is unwilling to tolerate an insult to his society. A person may be ready to forgive and forget a personal abuse to him, but the same man loses his temper if you abuse his society. It is possible that a person who is of a high character in his personal life, is unscrupulous as a member of society. Similarly, an individual can be good in his social life, but cannot be so in his personal life. This is a very important point.

Thinking Process of an Individual and a Society

If we analyse this situation, we shall discover that the modes of thinking of an individual and of a society are not always the same. These two do not bear an arithmetical relation. If a thousand good men gather together, it cannot be said for certain that they think similarly of good things.

An average Indian student at present is a mild and meek young man. Compared to an average student of twenty years ago, he is weaker and milder in every way. But when a score of such students get together, the situation becomes different. Then they indulge in all sorts of irresponsible actions. Thus a single student appears disciplined but a group of students becomes indisciplined. We shall have to consider why this change comes about. This is known as mob-mentality as distinct from individual mentality. This mob-mentality is a small aspect of mind. When a group of persons collect for a short time, the collective mentality obtained in that group is known as mob-mentality.

But society and social mentality evolve over a much longer period. There is a thesis that when people live together in a group for a long time, then by historical tradition and association and also by continued intercourse, they begin to think similarly and have similar customs. It is true that some uniformity is brought about by staying together. Friendship arises between two persons of similar inclination. However, a nation or a society does not spring up from mere co-habitation.

Why Mighty Nations of Antiquity Perished?

It is known that some ancient nations disappeared. The ancient Greek nation came to an end. Similarly, Egyptian civilisation disappeared. Babylonian and Syrian civilisations are a matter of history. Cynthians perished. Was there ever a time when the citizens of those nations stopped living together? It was only the fact that there were wide differences among the people that led to the downfall of these nations. Greece in the past produced Alexander and Herodotus, Ulysses and Aristotle, Socrates and Plato, and the present day Greece is inhabited by people of the same hereditary stock. There was no interruption in their heredity, because there never was a time when the whole of Greece was devoid of human population and when a new race inhabited that country. Such a thing never happened. Father and son tradition of old Greece was never interrupted. It is possible to trace the ancestry of present day Greeks to the old Greeks, some 250 to 500 generations back. Despite all this, the old Greek nation is non-existent. So also, the old Egyptian nation is no longer there. New nations have arisen in those places. How did this happen? This simple fact is indisputable that nations do not come into existence by mere co-habitation. There was never a time in the lives of the citizens of these decadent nations, when they stopped living in a group. On the other hand, Israeli Jews lived for centuries with other peoples scattered far and wide, yet they did not lose their identity in the societies in which they lived. It is clear, therefore, that the source of national feeling is not in staying on a particular piece of land, but in something else.

What is a Nation?

That source is in the goal which is put before the people. When a group of persons live with a goal, an ideal, a mission and look upon a particular piece of land as motherland, this group constitutes a Nation. If either of the two—an ideal and a motherland—is not there, then there is no Nation. There is a "Self" in the body, the essence of the individual; upon the severance of its relation with the body, a person is said to die. Similarly there is this idea, ideal, or fundamental principle of a Nation, it's soul. Although, it is believed that man takes birth again and again, yet the reborn person is a different individual. They are treated as two separate beings. The same soul leaves one body and enters another, but the former and the latter are two different individuals. The end of a person is nothing but the departure of his soul from his body. The other components of the body also undergo change. From childhood to old age, there is a drastic change. The biologists tell us that in the course of a few years, every cell of our body is replaced by a new one. A variety of changes takes place. Because the soul resides in the body without interruption the body continues its existence. Such a relation is known as 'the law of identity' in logic. It is due to this identity that we admit the continued existence of an entity. In this connection, a nice illustration of a barber's razor is sometimes advanced.

Once while shaving a customer, a barber prided in his razor being 60 years old. His father too had worked with the same razor. The customer was surprised, especially because the handle was quite shiny and new in appearance. "Why is the handle so shiny? How have you preserved the brightness for sixty years?" he asked. The barber too was amused with this. "Is it possible to preserve the handle in a brand new appearance for sixty years? It has been replaced only six months ago" he replied naturally. The customer was curious, and asked how old is the blade?" "Three years", was the reply. In brief, the handle was replaced, the blade was also replaced, but the razor remained old. Its identity was intact.

Similarly, a nation too has a soul. There is a technical name for it. In the "Principles and Policies" adopted by the Jana Sangh, this name is mentioned. The word is *Chiti* (चिति). According to McDougal, it is the innate nature of a group. Every group of persons has an innate nature. Similarly, every society has an innate nature, which is inborn, and is not the result of historical circumstances.

A human being is born with a soul. Human personality, soul and character are all distinct from one another. Personality results from a cumulative effect of all the actions, thoughts, and impressions of an individual. But the soul is unaffected by this history. Similarly, national culture is continuously modified and enlarged by historic reasons and circumstances. Culture does include all those things which, by the association, endeavours, and the history of the society, have come to be held as good and commendable, but these are not added on to *Chiti*. *Chiti* is fundamental and is central to the nation from its very beginning. *Chiti* determines the direction in which the Nation is to advance culturally. Whatever is in accordance with *Chiti* is included in culture.

By way of an illustration, consider the story of the Mahabharata. The Kauravas were defeated, and the Pandavas had won. Why did we hold the conduct of the Pandavas as *Dharma*? Or why was this battle not considered just a battle for a kingdom? The praise for Yudhisthira and the dishonour heaped on Duryodhana are not a result of political causes. Krishna killed his uncle Kansa, the established king of the times. Instead of branding this as a revolt, we consider Krishna as an *avatar* of God, and Kansa as an *asura*. Rama was assisted in his invasion of Lanka by Vibhishana, brother of Ravana, Such conduct of Vibhishana instead of being branded as treason, is considered good and exemplary. He betrayed his brother and his king, even as Jaichand had done later on. He might be branded as a "quisling". But Vibhishana is not called 'quisling" by anyone. On the contrary, he is praised highly for his conduct, and Ravana's actions are disapproved. Why is this so? The reason behind this is not political. If there is any standard for determining the merits and demerits of a particular action, it is this *Chiti*: whatever is in accordance with our nature or *Chiti* is approved and added on to the culture. These things are to be cultivated. Whatever is against *Chiti* is discarded as perversion, undesirable and is to be avoided. *Chiti* is the touchstone on which each action, each attitude is tested, and determined to be acceptable or otherwise. *Chiti* is the soul of the Nation. It is on the foundation of this *Chiti* (soul) that a Nation arises and becomes strong and virile. And it is this *Chiti* that is manifested in the action of every great man of a Nation. An individual is also an instrument in bringing forth the soul of the Nation *Chiti*.

Individual is also a tool to represent nation

Thus, apart from his own self, an individual also represents his Nation. Not only that but he also mans the various institutions that are created for the fulfillment of the national goal. Therefore he represents these too. The groups larger than Nation such as 'mankind' are also represented by him. In short, an individual has a multitude of aspects, but they are not conflicting; there is cooperation, unity and harmony in them. A system based on the recognition of this mutually complementary nature of the different ideals of mankind, their essential harmony, a system which devises laws, which removes disharmony, and enhances their mutual usefulness and cooperation, alone can bring peace and happiness to mankind, and can ensure steady development.

"Institution" – A Means to fulfil National Needs

According to Darwin's theory, living beings develop various organs as per the requirements dictated by the circumstances. In our *shastras*, it was stated slightly differently, that the soul constructs, using the strength of *prana*, various organs as the need is felt for the purpose of continuing life. Just as the soul produced these different organs in the body, so also in the Nation, many different organs are produced as instruments to achieve national goals. Like various departments in a factory, such as buildings, machinery, sales, production, maintenance, etc., nations also produce different departments which are called institutions. These institutions are created to fulfil the need of the Nation. Family, castes, guilds, (which are known as trade unions), etc. are such institutions. Property and marriage are also institutions.

Formerly there were no marriages. Later on, some *Rishi* established this practice of marriage. Similarly, *Gurukul* and *Rishikul* were institutions. In the same way, the State is also an institution. The Nation creates it. A lot of trouble in the West is due to the fact that they confused the State with the Nation, they considered the State synonymous with the Nation. Truly speaking, Nation and State are not the same. In our country, the State was produced as per the social contract theory. Formerly there was no State or king. The Mahabharata describes that in *Kritayuga*, there was no State or king. Society was sustained and protected mutually by practicing *Dharma*.

State and Society

Later on, interruption and disorganisation set in, greed and anger dominated. *Dharma* was on the decline and the rule of 'might is right' prevailed. The *Rishis* were perturbed over the developments. They all went to *Brahma* to seek counsel. *Brahma* gave them a treatise on 'Law and the Functions of the State', which he himself had written. At the same time he asked Manu to become the first king. Manu declined, saying that a king will have to punish other persons, put them in jail and so on; he was not prepared to commit all these sins. Thereupon Brahma said, "Your actions in the capacity of a king will not constitute sin, as long as they are aimed at securing conditions under which the society can live peacefully and according to *Dharma*. This will be your duty, your *Dharma*. Not only that, but you will also have a share of the *Karma* of your subjects, whereby you will gain *Dharma* considerably if your subjects maintain conduct according to *Dharma*". Although it is not explicitly stated here, I believe that if the society under any king committed sin, a part of that too, must automatically go to the account of the king. It is not proper if only good things are shared by the king and not the bad ones; both must be shared in the same proportion. Thus the State came into existence as a contract. This contract theory can be applied to the State, but not to the Nation. In the West, it was exactly opposite. Society as a Nation, according to them, was a contract, but the king claimed a divine right and proclaimed himself the sole representative of God. This is wrong. In our country, the king may have been first recognised in antiquity, but the society as a Nation is considered self-born. The State is only an institution.

Multiple Group Loyalties

Similarly, other institutions like the State, are created from time to time as the need is felt. Every individual is a limb of one or more of these institutions. A person is a member of his family as well as his community; he may also be a member of some association of his fellow professionals, if he pursues a profession. Above all, he is a member of the Nation and society. If we consider even the larger sphere, he is a member of the whole of mankind, and then the entire universe. Truly speaking, an individual is not merely a single entity, but a plural entity. He is a part of not just one, but a number of institutions. He lives a variety of lives. The most important is that, despite this multiple personality, he can and should behave in a way which does not bring different aspects of his life into mutual conflict, but which is mutually sustaining, complementary and unifying. This quality is inherent in man.

A person who uses this quality properly becomes happy. On the other hand, one who does not do so reaps unhappiness. Such a person will not have a balanced development in life. As an illustration, a man is the son of his mother, the husband of his wife, the brother of his sister, and the father of his son. A single individual is a father and also a son, he is a brother and also a husband. He has to maintain all these relations with intelligence, understanding and tact. Where a person fails to do so, there is conflict. If he sides with one party, the other feels wronged. The conflict between his wife and his sister, his wife and his mother, result from his inability to behave properly. Thereupon, some of his relations are strained. He is pained because his duties towards his mother and towards his wife clash. When he can resolve this conflict, and fulfil all his obligations properly, it can be said that his development will be integrated.

We do not accept the view that there is any permanent inevitable conflict among the multi-dimensional personality of an individual, and different institutions of the society. If a conflict does exist, it is a sign of decadence, perversion and not of nature or culture. The error in Western thinking lies in the fact that some people there believe that human progress is a result of this fundamental conflict.

Therefore, they consider the conflict between the individual and the State as a natural occurrence, and on the same basis they also theorised on the inevitability of class conflict.

Classes do exist in a society. Here too, there were castes, but we had never accepted conflict between one caste and another as a fundamental concept underlying it. The four castes, according to our conception, are thought of as analogous to the different limbs of the *Virat-Purusha*. It was suggested that the Brahmins were created from the head of the *Virat-Purusha*, the *Kshatriyas* from his hands, the *Vaishyas* from his abdomen and the *Sudras* from his legs. If we analyse this concept we are faced with the question of whether there can arise any conflict between the head, arms, stomach and legs of the same *Virat-Purusha*. If conflict is fundamental, the body cannot be maintained. There cannot be any conflict in the different parts of the same body. On the contrary, 'one man' prevails. The limbs are not only complementary to one another, but even further, there is individuality, unity. There is a complete identity of interests, identity of belonging. The origin of the caste system was on the above basis, and if this idea is not kept alive, the castes, instead of being complementary, can produce conflict. But then this is a distortion. It is not a systematic arrangement. Rather there is a lack of any plan, any arrangement. This is, indeed, the present condition of our society.

This process of deterioration can set in the various institutions of a society, due to a variety of reasons. If the soul of the society weakens, then all the different limbs of the society will grow feeble and ineffective. Any particular institution may be rendered useless or even harmful. Besides, the need and the usefulness of any particular institution may change with time, place and circumstances. While examining the present state of an institution, we ought, at the same time, to think of what it should be like. Mutual complementarity and a sense of unity alone can be the standard of proper conduct. Family, Community, Trade Union, *Gram Panchayat, Janapada,* State and such other institutions are various limbs of the Nation and even of mankind. They are interdependent, mutually complementary. There should be a sense of unity through all of them. For this very reason, there should be a tendency towards mutual accommodation in them, instead of conflict or opposition.

State is not Supreme

The State is one of several institutions, an important one, but it is not above all others (सर्वोपरि). One of the major reasons for the problems of the present-day world is that almost everyone thinks of the State to be synonymous with society. At least in practice, they consider the State as the sole representative of society. Other institutions have declined in their effectiveness, while the State has become dominant to such an extent, that all the powers are gradually being centralised in the State.

We had not considered the State to be the sole representative of the Nation. Our national life continued uninterruptedly even after the State went into the hands of foreigners. The Persian nation came to an end with their loss of independence. In our country, there were foreign rulers now and then in various parts of the country. At some time, the Pathans seized the throne of Delhi, and then the Turks, the Mughals and the British too established their rule. Despite all this, our national life went on, because the State was not its centre. If we had considered State as the centre, we would have been finished as a Nation long time ago. In some tales for children, it is described how an evil spirit resided in a parrot and to kill the evil spirit one had to kill that parrot. Those Nations whose life centred in the State were finished with the end of the State. One the other hand, where State was not believed central to its life, the Nation survived the transfer of political power.

This had its bad effects also. The late Dr. Ambedkar had said that our *Gram Panchayats* were so strong that we neglected the throne of Delhi. We did not remain alert as regards the State, as much as we ought to have done, thinking that Nation's life did not depend on the State. We forgot that, though it may be central, the State is definitely an important institution serving some needs of the Nation like a limb of the body. It is possible to pluck a hair without much harm, but along with the hair, if some skin is also removed, and a little further, if the head too is cut off, then there will be great loss for the body. Therefore, the body must be protected. Although the various limbs of the body are not absolutely indispensable, yet each of them serves an important purpose. From the same standpoint, State, too, should have been deemed important in the life of a Nation. There were persons who had paid attention to this aspect. It was for this reason that the great teacher of Shivaji, Samarth Ramdas Swami, directed him to establish his kingdom. *Dharma* wields its own power. *Dharma* is important in life. Shri Ramdas would as well have preached to Shivaji to become a mendicant and spread *Dharma* following his own example. But on the contrary, he inspired Shivaji to extend his rule, because State too is an important institution of society. However, to consider something important is different from saying that it is supreme (सर्वोपरि). The State is not supreme. The question arises, then, that if the State is not of fundamental importance, what is it that is absolutely important. Let us consider this question.

Dharma Sustains the Society

We shall have to examine the reasons why the State was established. No one will dispute that the State must have some specific aim, some ideal. Then this aim or ideal must be considered of highest importance, rather than the State which is created to fulfil this ideal. As a watchman is not deemed greater than the treasure he is supposed to protect, so is the case with the treasurer. The State is brought into existence to protect the Nation, and to produce and maintain conditions in which the ideals of the Nation can be translated into reality. The ideals of the Nation constitute *Chiti*, which is analogous to the soul of an individual. It requires some effort to comprehend *Chiti*. The laws that help manifest and maintain *Chiti* of a Nation are termed *Dharma* of that Nation. Hence, it is this *'Dharma'* that is supreme. *Dharma* is the repository of the Nation's soul. If *Dharma* is destroyed, the Nation perishes. Anyone who abandons *Dharma*, betrays the Nation.

Dharma is not confined to temples or mosques. Worship of God is only a part of *Dharma*. *Dharma* is much wider. In the past, temples had served as an effective medium to educate people in their *Dharma*. However, just as schools themselves do not constitute knowledge, so also temples do not constitute *Dharma*. A child may attend school regularly and yet may remain uneducated. So also, it is possible that a person may visit a temple or mosque without a break, and yet he may not know his *Dharma*. To attend a temple or mosque constitutes a part of a religion, sect, creed, but not necessarily *Dharma*. Many misconceptions have originated from faultly English translations, and the most harmful of them is due to the confusion of *Dharma* with religion.

Dharma and Religion are Different

On the one hand, we used the word religion as synonymous with *Dharma,* and on the other hand, increasing ignorance, neglect of our society and *Dharma,* and greater acceptance of European life, became the outstanding features of our education. As a result, all the characteristics of a narrow religion, especially as practiced in the West, were attributed automatically to the concept of *Dharma* also. Since in the West, injustice and atrocities were perpetrated, bitter conflicts and battles were fought in the name of religion, all these were listed *en bloc* on the debit side of

Dharma. We felt that in the name of *Dharma* also, battles were fought. However, battles of religion and battles for *Dharma* are two different things. Religion means a creed or a sect; it does not mean *Dharma*. *Dharma* is a very wide concept. It is concerned with all aspects of life. It sustains society. Even further, it sustains the whole world. That which sustains, is *Dharma*.

The fundamental principles of *Dharma* are eternal and universal. Yet, their implementation may differ according to time, place and circumstances. It is a fact that a human being requires food for maintaining his body. However, what a particular person should eat, in how much quantity, at what intervals, all these are decided according to circumstances. It is possible at times that even fasting is advisable. If a typhoid patient is given normal food, the consequences may be disastrous. For such a person, keeping away from food is necessary. Similarly, the principles of *Dharma* have to be adapted to changing times and place.

Some rules are temporary and others are valid for longer periods. There are some rules regulating our conduct at this meeting. One of the rules is that I speak and you listen to me with attention. If in contravention of this rule, you start conversing with one another or addressing the gathering at the same time, then there will be disorder; our work will not progress; the meeting will not be sustained. It can be said that you have not observed your *Dharma*. Thus it is our *Dharma* that we observe the rules by which the meeting proceeds smoothly. But this rule is applicable only as long as this meeting lasts. If the meeting is over and you do not speak even after reaching home, a different problem will crop up. Your family might have to call in a doctor. It is essential to observe the rules of the home once you reach there. The complete treatise on the rules in general, and their philosophical basis constitute what we mean by *Dharma*. These rules cannot be arbitrary. They should be such as to sustain and further the existence and progress of the entity which they serve. At the same time, they should be in agreement with, and supplementary to, the larger framework of *Dharma* of which they form a part. For instance, when we form a registered society, we have the right to frame the rules and regulations, but these cannot be contradictory to the constitution of the society. The constitution itself cannot violate the Societies Registration Act. The Act has to be within the provision of the constitution of the country. In other words, the constitution of the country is a fundamental document which governs the formulation of all acts in the country. In Germany, the constitution is known as the 'Basic Law'. Is the constitution too, not subject to some principles of a more fundamental nature? Or is it a product of any arbitrary decisions of a constituent assembly? On serious consideration, it will be clear that even the constitution has to follow certain basic principles of Nature. The constitution is for sustaining the Nation. Instead, if it is instrumental in its deterioration, then it must be pronounced improper. It must be amended. The amendment is also not solely dependent on majority opinion.

Nowadays, the majority is much talked of. Is the majority capable of doing anything and everything? Is the action of the majority always just and proper? No. In the West, the king used to be the sovereign. Thereafter when royalty was deprived of its so-called divine rights, sovereignty was proclaimed to be with the people. Here in our country, neither the kings, nor the people, nor the parliament have had absolute sovereignty. Parliament cannot legislate arbitrarily. It is said about the British Parliament that it is sovereign and can do anything. They say that "British Parliament can do everything except make a woman a man and vice versa" But is it possible for the Parliament to legislate that every Englishman must walk on his head? It is not possible. Can they pass an act that everyone in England must present himself before the local authority once everyday? They cannot. England has no written constitution. They have high regards for their tradition. But their traditions too have undergone change. What is the basis for making changes in their traditions? Whichever tradition proved an obstacle in the progress of England was discarded. Those which were helpful in the progress were consolidated.

Traditions are respected everywhere, just as in England. We have a written constitution, but even this written constitution cannot go contrary to the traditions of this country. In as much as it does go contrary to our traditions, it is not fulfilling *Dharma*. That constitution which sustains the Nation is in tune with *Dharma. Dharma* sustains the Nation. Hence we have always given prime importance to *Dharma,* which is considered sovereign. All other entities, institutions or authorities derive their power from *Dharma,* and are subordinate to it.

We need a Unitary Constitution

If we examine our Constitution from the point of view of the growth of the Nation, we find that our Constitution needs amendment. We are one Nation, one people. That is why we did not entertain any special rights on the basis of language, province, caste, religion, etc., but gave everyone equal citizenship. There are separate States. Yet there is no separate citizenship of State and of Union. We are all citizens of Bharat. By the same token, we have denied the right to secede to any individual State. Not only that, the power to demarcate the boundaries of States and to choose their names is vested in the Parliament and not in the Assemblies. This is as it should be, in tune with the nationalism and tradition of Bharat. However, despite all this, we made our Constitution federal, whereby what we have adopted in practice, we have rejected in principle. In a federation, the constituent units have their own sovereignty. But these powers are given to the Union. It has no power of its own. Thus the federal constitution considers the individual States as fundamental powers, and the Centre as merely a federation of States. This is contrary to the truth. It runs counter to the unity and indivisibility of Bharat. There is no recognition of the idea of *Bharatmata*, our sacred motherland, as enshrined in the hearts of our people. According to the first para of the Constitution "India that is Bharat will be a Federation of States", *i.e. Bihar Mata*, *Banga Mata*, *Punjab Mata*, *Kannada Mata*, *Tamil Mata*, are all put together to make *Bharatmata.* This is ridiculous. We have thought of the provinces as limbs of *Bharatmata* and not as individual mothers. Therefore, our Constitution should be Unitary instead of Federal.

Decentralisation of Power

A Unitary State does not mean concentration of all powers

in the Centre, just as the head of the family does not have all the powers with him even though all the transactions are carried out in his name. Others also share the executive powers. In our body also, does the soul possess all powers? Thus, a Unitary State does not mean a highly autocratic centre, nor does it entail the elimination of provinces. The provinces will have various executive powers. Even the various entities below the provincial level, such as the *Janapadas,* will have suitable powers. The *Panchayats* had a very important position. Nobody could dissolve *Panchayats*. Today, however, our constitution does not have any place for these *Panchayats*. There are no powers with these *Panchayats* in their own right. They exist at the mercy of the States only as delegated authorities. It is necessary that their powers be considered fundamental. In this way, the decentralisation of power will be accomplished. The authority will be distributed to the lowest level, and will be fully decentralised. At the same time, all those entities of power will be centred around the Unitary State. This arrangement will embody *Dharma*.

If we carry this concept of *Dharma* even further, not only the State and the Nation, but the nature of the entire mankind will have to be considered. In other words, the constitution of a Nation cannot be contrary to the natural laws. There are a number of norms of behaviour which are not found in any statute book, yet they do exist. At times, they are even stronger and more binding than any statutory law. The precept that one should respect one's parents is not written in any law. The present day governments which are turning out variety of laws, day in and day out, have not passed a law to this effect. Still, people respect their parents. Those who do not are criticised. If tomorrow there arises a discussion, even in a court, it will be generally accepted that as long as a person does not attain majority, he should accept his parents' decisions.

***Dharma* Means Innate Law**

Thus the fundamental law of human nature is the standard for deciding the propriety of behaviour in various situations. We have termed this very law as *Dharma*. The nearest equivalent English term for *Dharma* can be 'Innate law', which, however, does not express the full meaning of *Dharma.* Since *Dharma* is supreme, our ideal of the State has been *Dharma Rajya.* The king is supposed to protect *Dharma.* In olden times, at the coronation ceremony, the king used to recite three times – "There is no authority which can punish me". (A similar claim was made by kings in the Western countries, i.e. it was said, "King can do no wrong", and hence there too, nobody could punish the king). Upon this, the *purohit* used to strike the king on his back with a staff saying, "No, you are subject to the rule of *Dharma.* You are not sovereign." The king used to run around the sacred fire and the *purohit* would follow him striking him with the staff. Thus after completing three rounds, the ceremony would come to an end. Thereby, the king was unambiguously told that he was not an unpunishable sovereign. *Dharma* was above him. That is, even he was subject to *Dharma.*

Can the people do whatever they please? It may be contended that democracy means just that. The people can do what they please. But in our country, even if people wish, they are not free to act contrary to *Dharma.* Once a priest was asked, "If God is omnipotent, can he act contrary to *Dharma*? If he cannot, He is not omnipotent!" This was a dilemma. Can God practise *adharma* or is he not omnipotent? Actually God cannot act contrary to *Dharma.* If he does, then he is not omnipotent. *Adharma* is a characteristic of weakness, not of strength. If fire, instead of emitting heat, dies out, it is no longer strong. Strength lies not in unrestrained behaviour, but in well-regulated action. Therefore, God who is omnipotent is also self-regulated and consequently fully in tune with *Dharma.* God descends in human body to destroy *adharma* and re-establish *Dharma,* not to act on passing whims and fancies. Hence even God, who can do everything, cannot act contrary to *Dharma.* But, at the risk of being misunderstood, one can say that *Dharma* is even greater than God. The universe is sustained because he acts according to *Dharma.* The king was supposed to be a symbol of Vishnu, in as much as he was the chief protector of *Dharma Rajya.*

Dharma Rajya is not a Theocracy

Dharma Rajya does not mean a theocratic State. Let us be very clear on this point. Where a particular sect and its prophet or *guru* rule supreme, that is a theocratic State. All the rights are enjoyed by the followers of this particular sect. Others either cannot live in that country or at best, enjoy a slave-like, secondary-citizen's status. The Holy Roman Empire had this basis. The same concept was existing behind "*khilafat*". Muslim kings the world over used to rule in the name of *Khalifa*. After the First World War, this came to an end. Now efforts are afoot to revive it. Pakistan is the most recent theocratic State. They call themselves an Islamic State. There, apart from Muslims, all the rest are second-class citizens. Apart from this difference, there is no other sign of Islam in Pakistan's administration. The *Quran*, *Masjid*, *Roza, Id, Namaz*, etc., are the same both in Bharat, as well as in Pakistan. There is no need to tie up State and religion. By such a tie-up, there is no increase in an individual's capacity to worship God. The only result is that the State deviates from its duty. This does not happen in *Dharma Rajya*. Rather, there is freedom to worship according to one's own religion. In a theocratic State, one religion has all the rights and advantages, and there are direct or indirect restrictions on all other religions. *Dharma Rajya* accepts the importance of religion for peace, happiness and progress of an individual. Therefore, the State has the responsibility to maintain an atmosphere in which every individual can follow the religion of his choice and live in peace. The freedom to follow one's own religion necessarily requires tolerance for other religions.

We know that every kind of freedom has its inherent limits. I have the freedom to swing my hand, but as soon as there is a conflict between my hand and someone else's nose, my freedom has to be restricted. I have no freedom to swing my hand so as to hit another person's nose. Where another person's freedom is likely to be encroached upon, my freedom ends. The freedom of both parties has to be ensured. Similarly, every religion has the freedom to exist. But this freedom extends only as far as it does not encroach upon the religion of others. If such encroachment is carried on, it will have to be condemned as misuse of freedom, and will have to be ended. Such limitations will be required in all aspects of life. *Dharma Rajya* ensures religious freedom, and is not a theocratic State.

Nowadays the word 'Secular State' is being used as opposed to a theocratic State. The adoption of this word is a mere imitation of the Western thought-pattern. We had no need to import it. We called it a 'Secular State' to contrast it with Pakistan. There is some misunderstanding arising out of this. Religion was equated with *Dharma*, and then 'Secular State' was meant to be a State without *Dharma*. Some said, ours is a *Nidharma* State (*NiDharma*—without *Dharma*), whereas others trying to find a better sounding word, called it *'Dharmanirapekha'*—indifferent to *Dharma* State. But all these words are fundamentally erroneous. For a State can neither be without *Dharma* nor can it be indifferent to *Dharma*, just as the fire cannot be without heat. If fire loses heat, it does not remain fire any longer. A State which exists fundamentally to maintain *Dharma*, to maintain law and order, can neither be निधर्मी, (*NiDharmi*) nor धर्मनिरपेक्ष (*Dharmanirapekha*). If it is, निधर्मी, (*NiDharmi*), it will be a lawless State, and where there is lawlessness, where is the question of the existence of any State? In other words, the concept of *'Dharmanirapekshata'*—attitude of indifference towards *Dharma* and State are self-contradictory. State can only be '*Dharma Rajya*'—rule of *Dharma* and nothing else. Any other definition will go against the very *raison d'etre* of the State.

Legislature *versus* Judiciary

In a *Dharma Rajya*, the State is not absolutely powerful. It is subject to *Dharma*. We have always vested sovereignty in *Dharma*. Presently there has arisen a controversy. Whether the Parliament is sovereign or the Supreme Court, and whether the Legislature is higher or the Judiciary. This is like a quarrel as to whether the left hand is more important or the right hand? Both are the limbs of the State, the Legislature as well as the Judiciary. Both have distinct functions to perform. In their individual sphere, each is supreme. To consider either one above the other would be a mistake. Yet the legislators say, "We are higher". On the other hand, members of the Judiciary assert that they have a higher authority, since they interpret the laws which the Legislature makes. The Legislature claims to have given powers to the Judiciary. If necessary, the Legislature can change the Constitution. Hence it claims sovereignty. Now, since powers are bestowed by the Constitution, they are talking of amendments to the Constitution. But I believe that even if by a majority the Constitution is amended, it will be against *Dharma*. In reality, both the Legislature and the Judiciary are on an equal plane. Neither the Legislature is higher nor the Judiciary. *Dharma* is higher than both. The Legislature will have to act according to *Dharma,* and the Judiciary too, will have to act according to *Dharma*. *Dharma* will specify limits of both. The Legislature, the Judiciary or the people, none of these is supreme. Some will say "Why! People are sovereign. They elect." But even the people are not sovereign, because people too, have no right to act against *Dharma*. If an elected government allows people to go against *Dharma* and does not punish them, then that government is in reality a government of thieves. Even the general will cannot go against *Dharma*. Imagine what will be the situation, if by some manoeuvring, thieves gain a majority in the government and send one from their ranks as the head of executive. What will be the duty of the minority if the majority is of thieves and elects a thief to rule? The duty clearly will be to remove the representative elected by the majority.

Majority is not Always Right

During the Second World War, when Hitler attacked France, the French army could not stall the onward march of the Nazi troops. The then Prime Minister of France, Marshall Petain, decided to surrender. The French public supported the decision. But de Gaulle escaped to London where he declared that he did not accept the surrender. France is independent and will remain so. From London, he formed a Government of France in exile and eventually liberated France. Now if the majority rule is to be considered supreme, then de Gaulle's action will have to be condemned. He had no right to fight in the name of Independence. De Gaulle derived his right from the fact that the French nation was above the majority public opinion. The national *Dharma* is above all. Independence is *Dharma* for every Nation. It is the duty of every citizen to preserve its Independence, and to strive for regaining it when it is lost.

Even in our country, a majority had not risen against the Britishers; only a few had. Some revolutionaries sprang up, some brave people stood and fought. The Lokmanya declared, "Freedom is my Birthright". He did not declare this birthright with the support of a majority or a referendum of the people. Nowadays, people advocate that the merger of Goa should be decided by referendum, that there should be a plebiscite in Kashmir, etc., etc. This is wrong. National unity is our *Dharma*. A decision concerning this cannot be made by plebiscite. This type of a decision has already been taken by nature. Elections and the majority can only decide as to who will form the government. The truth cannot be decided by the majority. What the government will do, will be decided by *Dharma*.

You all know that in the U.S.A., where Americans swear by democracy, Lincoln did not accept the wrong public opinion on the question of the abolition of slavery. When the Southern states declared their intention to secede, Lincoln stood firm and told them: "You have no right to secede even in a democracy". He fought against this and did not allow them to secede. Nor did he tolerate slavery. He did not show readiness for a compromise whereby there might continue partial slavery to accommodate Southern states. He did not favour the policy of compromise. He categorically declared that the system of slavery was against tradition, the *Dharma*, the principles which were the basis of the American nation. Therefore the system of slavery had to be abolished. When the Southerners decided to secede, he told them, "You cannot secede". On this point, there was a civil war and Lincoln did not compromise with *adharma*.

Here in our country, the situation in this regard is very much like the old Hindu marriage, where a married couple could not divorce even if both the parties wished. The principle was that their behaviour should be regulated not by their sweet will but by *Dharma*. The same is the case with the Nation. If the four million people of Kashmir say that they want to secede, if the people of Goa say they want to secede or some say they want the

Portuguese to return – all this is against *Dharma*. Of the 450 million people of India, even if 449,999,999 opt for something which is against *Dharma*, this does not become the truth. On the other hand, even if one person stands for something which is according to *Dharma*, that constitutes the truth, because truth resides with *Dharma*. It is the duty of this one person that he treads the path of truth and changes people. It is from this basis that a person derives the right to proceed according to *Dharma*.

Let us understand very clearly that *Dharma* is not necessarily with the majority or with the people. *Dharma* is eternal. Therefore, it is not enough to say, while defining democracy, that it is the government of the people. It has to be a government for the good of the people. What constitutes the good of the people? It is *Dharma* alone which can decide. Therefore, a democratic government, *Jana Rajya*, must also be rooted in *Dharma,* i.e. *Dharma Rajya*. In the definition of democracy, *viz*. "government of the people, by the people and for the people" 'of' stands for independence, 'by' stands for democracy, and 'for' indicates *Dharma*. Therefore, there is true democracy only where there is freedom as well as *Dharma*. Rajya encompasses all these concepts.

24th April, 1965

□

Economic Structure Suited to National Genius

Yesterday we had discussed the functions of the State in a Nation. According to the *Bharatiya* traditions, a Nation is an organic living entity which has come into existence on its own and has not been made up of, or created by, any group of persons. A Nation brings forth a variety of institutions to fulfil its needs, as well as to give concrete shape to its inner fundamental nature. The State is one of these institutions, which, though an important institution, is not supreme.

In our ancient literature, wherever the duties of a king are referred to, his importance is definitely recognised. This is so, perhaps, to make him realise his immense responsibility. He exercises tremendous influence on the lives and character of the people. Hence, he has to give due attention to his own behaviour. Bhishma has said the same thing in the Mahabharata, when he was asked whether circumstances make a king, or a king makes the circumstances. He categorically stated that the king shapes the circumstances. Now some persons interpreted this to mean that he considered the king above all. But this is not true. He did not suggest that the king was above *Dharma.* It is true that the king wielded a great deal of influence, and that he was a protector of *Dharma* in society, but the king could not decide what constitutes *Dharma.* He only saw to it that people led their lives according to *Dharma.* In a way, he was equivalent to the present-day executive.

Responsibility of the Executive

In a modern state, the executive has the responsibility to execute the laws properly, but it does not enact laws. When the executive does not function with honesty and efficiency, the laws are entirely disregarded, as we may well see around us. And we can well say today, "Executive is responsible for the present evils to a great extent". After all why has prohibition failed? Who is responsible for its failure? When those very persons, who have been entrusted with the task of implementing prohibition, start taking monthly pay-offs from the bootleggers, how will the prohibition policy succeed? The executive is therefore, responsible for the proper enforcement of the law. This is the meaning of Bhishma's statement. It would be a mistake to interpret it as an acceptance of proven supremacy of a king. If this were so, how was it that the tyrant king Vena was removed by the *Rishis* and Prithu enthroned in his place? This action by the *Rishis* was never condemned by anyone in history. On the contrary, it was hailed by everyone. When the supremacy of *Dharma* is accepted as a principle, then through the authority of *Dharma,* the *Rishis* derive a right to remove a king who defaults in his duty. Otherwise, it would have been absolutely illegal to remove a king from his throne. Thus, if a king does not act according to *Dharma*, it becomes the duty of everyone to remove him. In Western countries, either a king was removed by some other king, or people rejected the sovereignty of the king altogether. Their king was a representative of God and could under no circumstances be removed at least in principle.

Various Institutions in the Social set up

In our socio-political set up, the king and the State were never considered supreme. Not only that, there were other important institutions (besides the State, which was only one of them) to regulate and to help carry on the social life. Those institutions had been organised both on a horizontal and vertical level, i.e. on regional and occupational basis. We had evolved *Panchayats* and *Janapada Sabhas*. The mightiest of the kings did not ever disturb the *Panchayats*. Similarly, there were associations on the basis of trade. These two were never disturbed by the State; on the contrary, their autonomy was recognised. They devised their own rules and regulations in their fields. The *Panchayats* of different communities, *shrenis, nigams*, Village *Panchayats,*

Janapada Sabhas and other such organisations, used to frame their own rules and regulations. The function of the State was mostly to see that these rules were observed by the persons concerned. The State never interfered with the affairs of these associations. Thus, the State was concerned only with some aspects of the life of the society.

Similarly, in the economic field, many institutions are created. We have to think what should be the nature of our economic structure. We must have such an economic system that helps in the development of our humane qualities or civilisation, and enables us to attain a still higher level of all-round perfection. We should have a system which does not overwhelm our humane quality, which does not make us slaves of its own grinding wheels. According to our concept, man attains God-like perfection as a result of development. Therefore, we have to devise such an economic system, to create such infrastructure and to frame such regulations, in which and by which, the inherent potentialities of man may find their highest fulfilment. Let us consider this point.

Limitation of Economic System

An economic system must achieve the production of all the basic things essential for the maintenance and development of the people, as well as the protection and development of the Nation. Having satisfied the basic minimum requirements, the question naturally arises whether there should be more production for greater prosperity and happiness. Western societies consider it most essential, and even desirable, to go on continuously and systematically increasing the desires and needs of man. There is no upper limit in this context. Normally, desire precedes the effort to produce the things desired. But now the position is reverse. People are induced to desire and use the things that have been or are being produced. Instead of producing to meet the demand, the search is on for markets for the goods already produced. If the demand does not exist, systematic efforts are made to create demand. This has become the chief characteristic of the Western economic system. Earlier, production followed the demand; now demand follows the production.

Consider the use of tea, for example. Tea was not produced because people desired and wanted it. But tea was produced and we were induced to develop a taste for tea. Now tea is a common man's drink. It has become a part of our life. The case of vegetable ghee is similar. Did anyone ever want to use it? It was first produced, and then we were taught to use it. If whatever is manufactured is not consumed, there will be depression. Some of us may remember the Great Depression of 1930-32. There was abundance of goods at that time, but there was no demand. Therefore, factories had to be closed down. Bankruptcy and unemployment were widespread. Thus nowadays, it is most important that what is being produced must be consumed.

The Editor of *Organiser*, an English Weekly, had gone to the U.S.A. for a visit sometime ago. Upon his return, he related an interesting instance. There is a factory which produces "Potato-peelers", a device for peeling potatoes. The production of this factory outstripped the demand for the device. The management of the firm faced the problem of finding some way by which people might be induced to buy more potato-peelers. They called a meeting of all the sales men of the firm. Among the suggestions put forward, one was to make the colour of the handle similar to that of potato peel, so that along with the peel, the peeler may also be dumped in the garbage, often by mistake. Thus, there may be greater demand. Also, the product was offered in a more attractive packing.

Do not Ignore Limitations of Nature

Now this economic structure is not merely consumption-oriented, but is clearly leading to destruction. Throw away the old one, and buy a new one! Rather than satisfying the need and demand of the people, to create fresh demand has become the aim of modern economics.

Taking Liberties with Nature

Supposing that we need not worry about the limited supply of natural resources, there is yet the question of balance in nature. There is a cyclic relationship in different parts of nature. If one of the three sticks, which stand with mutual support, is removed, the other two will automatically fall. The present economic system and system of production are fast disturbing this equilibrium of nature. As a result, on the one hand, new products are manufactured for satisfying ever increasing desires, and on the other hand, new problems arise every day, threatening the very existence of humanity and civilisation.

It is essential, therefore, to use up that portion of the available natural resources which nature itself will be able to recoup easily. When the fruits are taken, the fruit tree is not injured; it may even be helpful to the tree. However, in the effort to take a greater harvest from the land, chemical fertilisers are used, which in a few years' time, will render the land altogether infertile. Lakhs of acres of land lie barren in America due to this factor. How long can this dance of destruction go on?

The industrialist provides for a depreciation fund to replace machines when they are worn out. Then how can we neglect the depreciation fund for nature? From this point of view, it must be realised that the object of our economic system should not be to make extravagant use but a well-regulated use of available resources. The physical objects necessary for a purposeful, happy and progressive life must be obtained. The Almighty has provided that much. It will not be wise, however, to engage in a blind rat-race of consumption and production as if man is created for the sole purpose of consumption. Engine needs coal for its proper working, but it has not been produced merely to consume coal. On the contrary, it is only proper, always, to see that with the minimum coal consumption, maximum energy is produced. This is the economic viewpoint. Keeping in view the aim of human life, we must endeavour to see how, with the minimum of fuel, man proceeds to his goal with the maximum speed. Such a system alone can be called civilisation. This system will not think of merely a single aspect of human life, but of all its aspects, including the ultimate aim. This system will be constructive rather than destructive. This system will not thrive on the exploitation of nature, but will sustain nature, and will in turn itself be nourished. Milking, rather than exploitation, should be our aim. The system should be such that overflow from nature is used to sustain our lives.

Destructive Economic Slogans of the West

If such a human objective inspires the economic system, then our thinking on the economic questions will undergo thorough transformation. In the Western economies, whether it is capitalist or socialist, 'Value' has the most important and central position. All economic theories centre around 'Value'. It may be that the analysis of 'Value' is very important from the point of view of the economist, but those social philosophies which are based entirely on 'Value' are far more incomplete, inhuman and to some extent unethical.

Take for example, the slogan commonly heard nowadays, "One must earn his bread". Normally communists use this slogan, but even the capitalists are not fundamentally in disagreement with it. If there is any difference between them, it is only as regards who earns and how much. The capitalists consider capital and enterprise as important components of production, and hence if they take a major share of profits, they think it is their due. On the other hand, communists believe only labour to be the main factor in production. Therefore, they concede major share of production to the labourers. Neither of these ideas is correct.

Really speaking, our slogan should be that the one who earns will feed, and every person will have enough to eat. The right to food is a birthright. The ability to earn is a result of education and training. In a society, even those who do not earn must have food. The children and the old, the diseased and the invalids, all must be cared for by society. Every society generally fulfils this responsibility. The social and cultural progress of mankind lies in its readiness to fulfil this responsibility. The economic system must provide for this responsibility. The economic system must provide for this task. Economics as a science does not account for this responsibility. A man works not for bread alone, but also to shoulder this responsibility. Otherwise, those who have had their meals would no longer work.

Minimum Standard of Life

Any economic system must provide for the minimum basic necessities of human life to everyone. Food, clothing and shelter constitute, broadly speaking, these basic necessities. Similarly, society must enable the individual to carry out his obligations to society by educating him properly. Lastly, in the event of an individual falling prey to any disease, society must arrange for his treatment and maintenance. If a government provides these minimum requirements, then only it is a rule of *Dharma*. Otherwise, it is a rule of *adharma*. Describing King Dilip, Kalidas had said in *Raghuvansha*, "Being responsible for the maintenance, protection and education of his subjects, he was their true father. Others were merely instrumental in giving them their birth". The description of King Bharat after whom our country has been named Bharat, also runs similarly, i.e. "By maintaining and protecting his subjects, he was called Bharat". This is his country, Bharat. If in this country, maintenance and protection are not guaranteed, then the name Bharat is meaningless.

Education—A Social Responsibility

To educate a child is in the interest of society itself. By birth, a child is just like an animal. He becomes a responsible member of society only by education and culture. To charge fees for something which is in the interest of society itself, is rather odd. If due to their inability to pay the fees, children are left without an education, will the society be able to endure this situation for long? We do not charge fees from trees for sowing the seed and caring for the sapling. On the contrary, we invest our money and efforts. We know that when the tree grows, we shall reap fruits. Education is a similar investment. An educated individual will indeed serve society. On the other hand, it will not be surprising if people grow indifferent to society which leaves them to fend for themselves. Before 1947, in all the princely states in India, no fees were charged for education. The highest education was free. In the *Gurukuls,* even food and lodging were arranged without any charge. The student used to go to society for *Bhiksha*. No householder would refuse *Bhiksha* to the student. In other words, society used to bear the burden of education.

Similarly, it is rather surprising that one has to pay for his medical treatment. In fact, medical treatment also should be free as it was in this country in the past. Nowadays, one has to pay even to get an entrance to a temple! There is a charge of twenty-five paise to enter to enter the Balaji temple at Tirupati. However, there is a *Dharma darshan* at noon for one hour, during which period the payment of charges is not required. At other times it is as though *adharma darshan*, when charges are to be paid. The society should guarantee to all its members, minimum requirements for maintenance and progress of every individual. Now the question arises, if everyone is to be guaranteed the minimum necessities, where will the resources for all this come from?

Minimum Standard of Living : A Birth Right

It is clear that the resources must be produced by our own efforts. Therefore, where a right to a guaranteed minimum is recognised, any individual who does not share in the efforts to produce is a burden to society. Similarly, any system which obstructs the production activity of the people is self-destructive. Such a system will not enable individuals to fulfil their responsibilities. Not only that, but even if the requirements of an individual are met, while he does not share in the efforts, his personality will not develop fully, and his progress as a human being will be distorted and lopsided.

Man has a stomach as well as hands. If he has no work for his hands, he will not get happiness even if he gets food to satisfy his hunger. His progress will be obstructed. Just as a barren woman experiences emptiness in life and consequent dissatisfaction, so does a man without work.

The guarantee of work to every able-bodied member of society should be the aim of our economic system. Today we witness a very strange situation. On the one hand, a ten year old child and a seventy-year old man are toiling and on the other hand a youth of twenty-five is driven to suicide for want of work. We shall have to remove this mismanagement. God has given hands to every man, but hands by themselves have a limited capacity to produce. They need the assistance of capital in the form of machines. Labour and capital bear the same relation to each other as that between man and nature. The world is a creation of these two. Neither of them can be neglected.

Capital Formation

For capital formation, it is essential that a part of production be saved from immediate consumption, and be used for further production in future. Thus, capital can be formed only by restraint on consumption. This is the basis of capital formation to which Karl Marx refers to as 'surplus value' in his treatise. In the capitalist system, the industrialist creates capital with the help of this surplus value. In a socialist system, the State undertakes this task. In both the systems, the entire production is not distributed among the workers. If production is carried on through centralised large-scale industries, the sacrifice on the part of the worker in creating the capital is not given due recognition. The advantage in decentralisation is in the fact that the worker has a sense of direct participation in the management of the surplus value or capital.

Super Money of Machine Over Man

Machines are the most common form of capital. Machines were created in order to reduce the content of physical labour in production and to increase the productivity of the worker. Machines, therefore, are an assistant of the worker and not his competitor. However, where the human labour came to be considered as a commodity to be purchased with money, the machine became the competitor of the human being. The principal drawback of the capitalist viewpoint lies in the fact that by making the machine a competitor of human labour, and thereby displacing and subjecting a human being to deprivation privations, the very purpose of creating machines has been defeated. Machines cannot be blamed for this. It is the fault of the economic and social system which cannot distinguish between the object and the instrument. It is only after considering the limitations of the machine that one has to decide upon its usefulness. From this point of view, to import machinery from Western countries, where shortage of manpower was the guiding factor in the design of machines, would be a serious mistake. The merits of machines are not independent of time and place. Machines are a product of modern science but not its representatives. Scientific knowledge is not a monopoly of any particular country. But its application has to take into account the particular condition of each country and its requirements. Our machines must not only be tailored for our specific economic needs, but must also, at least, avoid conflict with our socio-political and cultural objectives.

The Seven M's

Professor Visweswarayya has said in one of his books that, while considering the system of production, one must take into account the seven M's. These are man, material, money, management, motive power, market and machine. The skill and ability of the workers or those who should be provided work must be considered. Easy availability of the required raw material, and the quality and properties of the raw material available cannot be ignored. We must also think of how much money is available as capital. How this capital can be increased and at what rate? How best can it be utilised for maximum production? How much of it should be put in fixed assets and how much should be kept in liquid form? We must also pay attention to the forms of power available in the country, in addition to the human and animal labour. Wind, water, steam, oil, gas, electricity and atomic power can supply the motive power. Of these, which form of power can be obtained, in what quantity without being uneconomic, must be thought of while deciding upon our methods of production. In the same way, managerial skills are also important and deserve due attention. If the ability to co-ordinate the efforts of a dozen workers is wanting, all of them will remain unemployed. It is also necessary to think of the usefulness of the goods produced to the society. This means that production of any particular commodity cannot be justified economically without the consideration of the market it commands. Taking into consideration all these factors we should design suitable machines. Instead, we find nowadays, that we install the machines first and try to coordinate all other factors afterwards. Other countries of the world did not progress in this fashion. Otherwise, new machines would not have been invented. We are importing the machine and hence we have little knowledge. We shall have to develop a *Bharatiya* technology.

None of the seven factors is unchangeable. In fact, each one keeps constantly changing. Those who are entrusted with the task of planning, must think of how the change is directed towards progress, how physical hardship is reduced, and waste of energy is minimised. As an illustration, let us take the low productivity of our worker. It can be increased by using machines, and it is necessary to do so. But if the machine is such that the requires only a few men to run it, then the rest of the people will be thrown out of employment. If the machine has to be imported from other countries at such a heavy cost, that the additional production it causes will be insufficient to make it economic, then such a machine is not suitable to our requirements. Just as to let a part of the installed capacity of a factory remain unutilized, is a losing proposition, so also to let the people of this country remain unemployed is a losing proposition. Nay, this is even worse. Whereas a machine eats up only the capital invested in it in the past, the unemployed people have to be fed, which is a continuous and unending drain on resources, consumed at double the speed. Therefore, instead of the usual exhortation of "Every worker must get food" we must think of "Everyone who eats must get work", as the basis of our economy. No doubt the *charkha* has to be replaced by machines, but not necessarily automatic machines everywhere. Full employment must be a primary consideration, and then the rest of the six factors suit this.

Man's Place in the Capitalist System

The use of manpower and the employment question will have to be thought of in the context of the human being as a whole, as an integral being. The economic theories of the past few centuries and the structure of society based on these theories, are such that there has been a thorough devaluation of the human being. His personality is altogether irrelevant to the economic set up. A capitalist economy recognises only an 'economic man', whose decisions are all based entirely on calculations of gain and loss, in terms of material wealth. For this economic man, five rupees are always more than four rupees. He works solely to gain more wealth, and exerts himself to get the maximum gain. For him, just like other commodities, human labour is a commodity to be bought and sold in the market. This is free enterprise. It holds all other restrictions and regulations unjust, save the brake of competition. In the race, no one is prepared to stop and give a helping hand to the weak who is left behind; nay, elimination of the weak is considered just and natural. He is an uneconomic, marginal unit, not fit to exist. This is what it advocates. By the elimination of such marginal units, the economic power accumulates in the hands of a few. This is considered normal and natural in a capitalist system. But when monopoly is established, even the check of competition ceases to operate. In such a situation, the incentive resulting from competition is no longer available. Prices are arbitrarily fixed and the quality of products deteriorates.

Even as regards the consumer's needs, the capitalist is guided not by the necessities and desires of the consumer, but by his purchasing power. The needs of the wealthy and well-fed are attended to, rather than those of the poor and the hungry. As a result, where countless varieties of goods are produced for the needs of the wealthy, even the basic necessities of life for the poor become scarce.

No Development Possible under the Capitalist System

The centralisation and monopolisation of production totally undermine the influence of the consumer. The markets are so organised that the consumer has to go for standard products. This standardisation is on the increase at such a pace, that individual preference of the consumer is ignored. Like the books in the library, even human beings are allotted numbers as consumers. The system which boasts of giving highest importance to the individual, has ironically destroyed all individuality. Clearly, the capitalist system is incapable of helping the development of an integral human being.

Socialist System is a Reaction

Socialism arose as a reaction to capitalism. But even socialism failed to establish the importance of the human being. Socialists contended themselves by merely transferring the ownership of capital in the hands of the State. But the State is even more of an impersonal institution.

All the business of the State is conducted by rigid rules and regulations. Generally, there is no place for individual discretion, and even where such discretion is allowed, the slightest laxity in the sense of duty and social responsibility on the part of the administrators, results in corruption and favouritism.

The capitalistic system thought merely of the economic man, but left him free in other fields where he could exercise his individuality. The socialist system went much further, and thought only of the 'abstract man'. After that, there was no scope for the development of the individual's personality based on diverse tastes and abilities. The needs and preferences of individuals have as much importance in the socialist system as in a prison manual. There is no such thing as individual freedom in the socialist system.

State over powers the individual

There is no private property in a socialist society. This removes the problems accompanying the institution of private property. However, the incentive for production and conservation of resources, and economy in utilisation, accompany the institution of private property. There has been no alternative arrangement to preserve these. The State is made supreme and the sole authority in all matters. The individual citizen is reduced to a mere cog in this giant wheel. There is no provision to inspire the individual to fulfil his role. As Djilas states, "The class of old fashioned exploiters has been eliminated, but a new class of bureaucratic exploiters has come into existence". Karl Marx put forward, in his analysis of history, that capitalism contains the seeds of its own destruction, and that communism is a natural and inevitable successor to capitalism.

This concept may be helpful in fostering faith in the communists about their ultimate victory, but certainly such a determinist view destroys the urge for reform and dynamism in man. He is no longer the creator of a new order; he is merely incidental to a predetermined historical process. His task is only to accelerate the process. Therefore, even as he tries to organise workers, he cares little for their welfare, but uses them as mere tools for the revolution. The dialectic materialism of Marx, too, operates only so long as the State is not established as supreme after destroying the capitalists. Thereafter, the State puts a stop to the operation of the principle of dialectic materialism. In the name of crushing the counter-revolutionaries, the State becomes more and more totalitarian. The day when the State is to wither away, yielding place to a stateless society remains a mere dream. In fact, according to the Marxist view, to obstruct the process of thesis, anti-thesis and synthesis is in itself reactionary. Marx is thus falsified by his own standards.

Both these systems, capitalist as well as communist, have failed to take account of the 'Integral Man', his true and complete personality and his aspirations, One considers him a mere selfish being hankering after money, having only one law, the law of fierce competition, in essence the law of the jungle; whereas the other has viewed him as a feeble lifeless cog in the whole scheme of things, regulated by rigid rules, and incapable of any good unless directed. The centralisation of power, economic and political, is implied in both. Both, therefore, result in the dehumanisation of man.

Man, the highest creation of God, is losing his own identity. We must re-establish him in his rightful position, bring him to the realisation of his greatness, re-awaken his abilities and encourage him to exert for attaining divine heights of his latent personality. This is possible only through a decentralised economy.

We want neither capitalism nor socialism.

We aim at the progress and happiness of 'Man', the Integral Man. The protagonists of the two systems fight with Man on the stake. Both of them do not understand Man, nor do they care for his interest.

The objectives of our economy should be:

1. An assurance of the minimum standard of living to every individual and preparedness for the defence of the Nation.
2. Further increase above this minimum standard of living whereby the individual and the Nation acquire the means to contribute to world progress on the basis of its own *Chiti*.

3. To provide meaningful employment to every able-bodied citizen, by which the above two objectives can be realised, and to avoid waste and extravagance in utilising natural resources.
4. To develop machines suited to *Bharatiya* conditions (*Bharatiya* technology), taking note of the availability and nature of the various factors of production (Seven Ms).
5. This system must help, and not disregard the human being—the individual. It must protect the cultural and other values of life. This is a requirement which cannot be violated except at the risk of great peril.
6. The ownership, state, private or any other form, of various industries must be decided on a pragmatic and practical basis.

These are few general directions which we must bear in mind while developing our economy. *Swadeshi* and 'Decentralisation' are the two words which can briefly summarise the economic policy suitable for the present circumstances. Centralisation and monopolisation have been the order of the day for all these years, knowingly and unknowingly. The planners have become prisoners of a belief that only large-scale, centralised industry is economic, and hence, without worrying about its ill-effects, or knowingly but helplessly, they have continued in that direction. The same has been the fate of *Swadeshi*. The concept of *Swadeshi* is ridiculed as old-fashioned and reactionary. We proudly use foreign articles. We have grown over-dependent upon foreign aid in everything from thinking, management, capital, methods of production, technology, etc., to even the standards and forms of consumption. This is not the road to progress and development. We will forget our individuality and become virtual slaves once again. The positive content of *Swadeshi* should be used as the cornerstone for the reconstruction of our economy.

Usher in the new era

For want of time, I have not touched upon the natural aspects of economic structure. But one thing is clear—that many old institutions will yield place to new ones. This will adversely affect those who have vested interests in the old institutions. Some others who are by nature averse to change will also suffer by efforts of reconstruction. But disease must be treated with medicine. Strength can be gained only from exercise and hard work. Therefore, we shall have to discard the *status quo* mentality and usher in new era. Indeed our efforts of reconstruction need not be clouded by prejudice or disregard for all that is inherited from our past. On the other hand, there is no need to cling to past institutions and traditions which have outlived their utility. We have considered what the direction of change should be.

Epilogue

We have, in the last four days, thought over the integrated form of Humanism. On this basis, we shall be able to re-reconcile nationalism, democracy, socialism and world peace with the traditional values of *Bharatiya* culture and think of all these ideals in an integrated form. The mutual conflict among these ideals can be removed and they can supplement mutually. Thereby 'Man' can gain his lost status and attain the aims of his life.

We have discussed here the philosophy. But the members of Bharatiya Jana Sangh are not mere philosophers or academicians. We have set out with the determination to make this Nation strong, happy and prosperous through the medium of the Bharatiya Jana Sangh. Therefore, we must carry on practical programmes for the national reconstruction on this foundation. We have taken due note of our ancient culture. But we are no archaeologists. We have no intention to become custodians of a vast archaeological museum. Our goal is not merely to protect the culture but to revitalise it so as to make it dynamic and in tune with the times. We must ensure that our Nation stands firm on this foundation and our society is enabled to live a healthy, progressive and purposeful life. We shall have to end a number of traditions and set in reforms which are helpful in the development of values and of national unity in our society. We shall remove those traditions which obstruct this process. Whereas one need not mourn the limitations of the human body, one must undergo the required surgical operation if any part of the body has a cancerous growth. There is no need to amputate healthy limbs. If today, society is gripped with evils like untouchability, which leads men to treat other human beings as lower than themselves, and thereby threaten the national unity, we shall have to end such evils.

We shall be required to produce such institutions as will kindle the spirit of action in us, which will replace the self-centredness and selfishness by a desire to serve the Nation, which will produce not only sympathy towards our brethren, but a sense of affection and oneness with them. Such institutions can truly reflect our *Chiti*.

Chiti is a Nation's soul. The power that energises and activates the Nation is called *Virat*, which in turn is aroused and organised and canalised by *Chiti*. The place of *Virat* in the life of a Nation is similar to that of *Prana* in the body. Just as *Prana* infuses strength in various organs of the body, refreshes the intellect, and keeps body and soul together, so also in a Nation, with a strong *Virat* alone, can democracy succeed and the government be effective. Then the diversity of our Nation does not prove an obstacle to our national unity. The differences of language, occupation, etc., are present everywhere. However, when the *Virat* is awake, diversity does not lead to conflict and people co-operate with one another like the various limbs of the human body or like the members of a family.

We have to undertake the task of awakening our Nation's *Virat*. Let us start carrying on this task of awakening the *Virat* of the Nation with a high sense of pride in our hoary glorious past, taking a realistic assessment of the present and having a great ambition for the future. We wish neither to make this country a shadow of some distant past nor an imitation of Russia or America.

With the support of universal knowledge and our heritage, we shall create a Bharat which will excel all its past glories, and will enable every citizen in its fold to develop his manifold latent potentialities and to achieve, through a sense of unity with the entire creation, a state even higher than that of a complete human being. It is a state in which *Nar* (Man) becomes *Narayan (God). This is the eternal and continuous divine form of our culture. This is our message to humanity at the crossroads. May God give us the strength to succeed in this task.*

BHARAT MATA KI JAI

25th April, 1965

□

Presidential Speech at Calicut in Kerala in December 1967
V.N. Deodhar

Fellow delegates,

You have entrusted to me this year the responsibility of party presidentship. Ours is an organization of workers, all engrossed in building up the party with equal zeal and devotion. That you have called upon me to fulfil this particular constitutional obligation and thus honoured me, is token only of your own generosity and affection, which indeed I have been receiving in liberal measure during the past fifteen years that I have been General Secretary. It is this generous affection of all of you that is going to be my mainstay hereafter too.

Conjunction of Two Eras

We are meeting today in Kerala, this land hallowed by Bhagwan Parashuram's *tapas*. In point of time we are at the conjunction of two years. During the half century gone by, the country's mind has been dominated completely by the Congress and its ideology. Its leaders have been not only the framers of national policy but the arbiters of contemporary life-values as well. After independence, the reins of government also came into their hands. While this is no occasion for any elaborate stock-taking of the Congress's performance, it cannot be gain–said that awakening of political consciousness in the common man has been the most significant contribution of this era. If this political consciousness, unpolluted by the exigencies of the day-to-day politics, had been made an instrument for the country's resurgence on a positive national basis, we would have made considerable progress by now and the country might have been spared the problems which beset it today. The new era, at whose threshold the country stands today, should be a positive manifestation of this political awakening. There are people in the country who are still chained to the age gone by. Then there are others who are ignorant of national values, or have scant regard for them, and so are readily influenced by foreign concepts. The country's transition into the new era, therefore, is not being smooth. It is accompanied by severe strains and struggles. It is against this background that we must analyze present problems and draw up our policy.

Search for an Alternative

Portents of the coming revolution had become visible in August-September 1965, when India's brave legions proved their valour against Pakistani aggression. The policies framed by the Congress regime in wake of these events demonstrated only its utter incapacity to function as the instrument of the coming revolution. The result was that the people began longing all the more intensely for emancipation from Congress misrule. With the Fourth General Election, the process has started for Congress's gradual withering away. If opposition parties had been better organised then, the results would have been even more convincing. In comparison to other parties the Jana Sangh's achievement in the election have been considerably significant. But in relation to the demands of the situation, the results left much to be desired. However, the outcome of these elections clearly proved to the people the Jana Sangh's potential of growing into a clear alternative to the Congress. It is this confidence created in the people which accounts for the sharp rise in the party's popularity and its organizational expansion after the election.

Nature of Problems

Post-election problems can be classified into three categories. Firstly, there are the problems pertaining to the politics of the transition. Inter-party relations, instability of coalition ministries, floor-crossing etc. are problems which fall in this category. To the second category belong those problems which stem from our constitutional set-up but which had either not arisen as yet, or had not confronted us as seriously as now. And thirdly, there are the manifold problems relating to economic, defence, home and foreign affairs which, because of the impolicies of the Congress Government, have become very grave now. Problems of the first category are of immediate topical interest and so generally evoke the maximum of public comment and debate. But they are less important than those in the other two categories. If these letter problems are not properly tackled, they can jeopardise the country's unity and interests seriously.

Conduct of Governors

The first problem which faced opposition parties after the elections was that except in Delhi and Madras, nowhere else was any single party able to secure a clear majority and so be able to form an alternative non-Congress Government by itself. Appreciating the requirements of the situation and in deference to the verdict of the electorate various non-Congress parties came together to form coalition governments in Punjab, Bihar, West Bengal and Kerala. In Rajasthan and Uttar Pradesh, however, in the teeth of public opposition, the Congress contrived to worm its way into office with the assistance of the State Governors. In Uttar Pradesh they could not hold on to office for long; but in Rajasthan, by taking recourse to various devious means, they have managed to increase their majority considerably.

The arbitrary conduct of the Governors in the above cases, then later in Madhya Pradesh at the time of the fall of the Mishra

Government, and again recently in West Bengal, Haryana and Punjab, has lowered the prestige of this august once and weakened regard for constitutional proprieties. As Governors are the representatives of the Centre, the Central Government must own full responsibility for their actions. By declining to take the onus of their actions the Central Government has only created mistrust about its own *bona fides* and confirmed misgivings that they are intent on using the office of Governor only as a facade behind which they might further their own party ends.

The demand has been voiced in some quarters that the Governor's should be an elected post. I do not think that would solve the problem. Exceptional occasions apart, the Governor is only a constitutional head. Appointees to this post, therefore, should be men of integrity capable of exercising their discretion in a judicious manner and in whose impartiality there is general confidence. I think that it would be better if instead of selecting rejected politicians or retired civil servants for this job, the Government turned its eyes to retired judges of the Supreme Court. A list may be drawn up on the basis of their dates of retirement and posts of Governors falling vacant here' after may be filled by these judges in their order of priority. If some such convention is followed, neither the consent of the State Government concerned, nor the wishes of the Home Ministry would have any relevance.

Performance of Coalition Governments

On the administrative level, the coalition governments did present a better alternative to the Congress, but they did not over any comprehensive set of policies and programmes in substitution of the Congress's. Actually, I thinks, they were not intended to. It is a matter of regret that some of the constituents of these coalitions failed to appreciate the ideological limitations under which such coalitions would necessarily have to function, and tried to use these governments as instruments for the execution for their respective party policies. As the result of this partisan approach and lack of a sense of responsibility, these governments have been subjected to internal strains, and have had always to work under a shadow of uncertainty. It must be recorded, however, that despite all these handicaps, despite the limited resources and rights of the

States, and despite continuing Central machinations to topple non-Congress governments, these coalitions have during their brief term of office brought relief to the people in many matters. Of course, they who expected these governments to work miracles might have been disappointed.

If this coalition experiment has given birth to a sense of realism and a habit of objective political appraisal, that, in itself, would be a gain. Also, the formation of these Governments has been a commendable step in the direction of eradicating political untouchability. A readiness to appreciate an opponent's viewpoint and a willingness on the part of different parties to work together in spite of variations of policy is an index of a democratic temperament and of the nation's basic homogeneity. Whatever be the future of these coalition governments, I wish we are able to conserve this achievement.

Parliamentary Democracy on Trial

The strains inside these coalitions and the political instability resulting from the continued efforts to topple these Governments, or from their fall, have prompted many to suggest that the present cabinet form of Government are discarded in favour of the Presidential system. Shri Ashok Mehta has suggested that the system be introduced only at the State level. I really fail to understand why a distinction is sought to be made between the Centre and the States. Fact is that the systems of Government in Britain and in the U.S.A. have grown out of their history. Instead of trying merely to imitate the one or the other, let us try to evolve democratic practices suited to our own genius. Actually, during the past 50 years or so we have been working with the parliamentary system of Government. It would be more fruitful if we try to mould this to suit our changing politics. Instead of conventions relevant to the two party democracy of the British Parliament, let us develop conventions suited to the multi-party

pattern of Indian politics so that the instability of the transition period can be avoided. A convention can be accepted, for instance, that no Government would resign except on the adoption of a no-confidence vote against it by the legislature. Another convention which might be evolved in conjunction with the above one is that if a majority of the members of a legislature request the Speaker that the House be convened; a meeting of the legislature would be invariably summoned.

Problem of Floor-Crossing

Floor-crossing by legislators is another issue which has occasioned much comment in the context of the formation and fall of Governments lately. Floor-crossing is no new phenomenon. Quitting the Congress on the eve of elections and rejoining it after the elections has been a familiar feature of Indian politics and the birth of several parties and the dissolution of others can be traced to this feature. Even those who may not have left the Congress have been shifting their factional loyalty within the party very frequently. As a result of all this even though, outwardly, the Congress's name has been a constant, Congress Ministries have been in a state of perpetual instability and have often fallen too. After independence Congress and Congressmen have betrayed a singular idealism and direction. It is, therefore, that they have been inclined to behave thus. Ninety-nine per cent of those guilty of floor-crossing are either Congressmen or ex-Congressmen. As the policies and programmes of parties crystallize on the basis of well defined principles, their organisations become stronger and political enlightenment of the masses grows and enables talent to exercise their vote on the basis of a party's platform, this tendency of floor-crossing will automatically decline.

It has been suggested that legislative steps be opportunistic floor-crossing. Rather than take recourse to law to control law-makers, it would be better to leave the matter to convention and the pressure of public opinion. After all, every legislator is responsible not only to his party but to his constituency and the country as well. It would not be easy to fit all these varied obligations of his into a rigid legal scheme. If, however, political parties could agree on a code of conduct in this regards opportunism can be suitably checked. Also, if instead of having electors vote for individual candidates on the British pattern, we could have the Lists System in which votes are cast for the party, many of the evils of present-day politics might be obviated. Perhaps, a synthesis of both these patterns on the lines of West Germany might suit us best.

Centre-States Relations

The Congress continues to rule at Centre while in the States we have several non-Congress Governments. This has invested the issue of Centre-States relations with considerable political importance. Our Constitution is federal in form but most of its provisions reveal a unitary bias. The political situation prevailing during the last 20 years and the existing planning and financial arrangements have made the Centre all the more powerful. In the past, as the Congress held away at all levels, no one ever challenged the Centre's dominance or alleged misuse of authority by the Centre. The Congress High Command also exercised its influence to see that Centre-State relations remained smooth. The situation has now changed, however. Several States are now in the hands of non-Congress Governments. They wish to serve the people according to their own concept. They should be given a full opportunity to do so, and provided resources to meet their obligations.

The sovereign authority of the nation vests in the Central Government. In its dealings with the State Governments, let the Central Government show an awareness of this responsibility, and act in a liberal and impartial manner. If, instead, they keep looking at things from the narrow party standpoint and try to explain away pettiness of approach by citing powers conferred on them by the Constitution, they would only be harming the country's interests. Nationalists would feel sore and frustrated while those interested in promoting disintegration and disruption would exploit the situation only to challenge and weaken the Centre's authority. The conduct of Communists in West Bengal and Kerala is a pointer. In order that Centre-States tensions should not imperil the country's unity, it is necessary that while on the one hand the structure of our Constitution is made unitary, on the other, financial and other powers presently concentrated in the Centre should be decentralised in favour of the States to enable them discharge their functions responsibly.

Wanted: Permanent Finance Commission

Financially, the States today are badly dependent, on the Centre. The Constitution so divides resources and obligations between the Centre and the States that the entire burden of Administration, Public Welfare and Development lies on the States while all the elastic and rich resources of revenue are with the Centre. Although States do get a share of Income tax and Excise duty on the basis of recommendations made by the Finance Commission, they have to depend very greatly on discretionary grants from the Centre. In 1951-52, 29.4 per cent of the States' expenditure came from Central resources. According to the revised figures for 1966-67, this amount has risen to 55.3 per cent. Over the same period the Centre's discretionary grants to the States have risen from 7 per cent to 19 per cent of the States' expenditure. Obviously, this state of affairs militates against the spirit of responsible government. It has to be changed. A demand is being made that the Constitution should be amended for the purpose. I think that without amending the Constitution, a flexible arrangement can be devised to meet the requirements of the changed situation. The Finance Commission, which is now appointed every five years, can be made a permanent body, and grants and loans under Article 282 given by the Central Government in its own discretion may be brought within the purview of the Commission's recommendations.

Tax-Structure Needs Re-Examination

In the same context, it needs to be observed that States also should consider how fully to exploit their own resources. No doubt, there is a need to lessen the tax burden and to simplify the existing machinery for tax realisation. But I must say that the present taxation policies of several State Governments bear the impress more of political slogans than of Governmental responsibility. Many revolutionary ideas are now being propounded in respect of land revenue; income tax, sales tax etc. It would be well if all these proposals are submitted to scientific scrutiny before a final decision is taken in their regard because these taxes have been till now important sources of revenue.

Even otherwise, there is imperative need for a Commission to examine the entire tax structure. It was in 1953-54 that the last Taxation Enquiry Commission had been constituted. The first Plan had only been launched then. Now, three Plans have been completed. In 1951-52, the total tax revenue of the Centre and the States was Rs. 638 crores whereas the estimated tax-revenue for 1967-68 is Rs. 3599 crores. During this period land-revenue has been doubled, income tax and company tax quadrupled, sales tax increased 9 times and excise duty 18 times. These taxes have off and on been increased on an *ad hoc* basis and later the increase has been made permanent. Again, there are commodities which have been subjected to excise duty, sales tax as well as octroi duties and terminal taxes. This has naturally increased their price. During the last 15 years there have been vast changes in the distribution of incomes. The value of the Rupee has gone down steeply, States have been reorganised and today the Plan itself is being reconsidered. Because of all these consideration, appointment of Taxation Enquiry Commission is necessary. This Commission might consider all problems of economic development, capital formation, public welfare, the need to remove disparities and the requirements of decentralised government, and in that light make recommendations about existing taxes and the tax Structure.

Devaluation Has Halted Economy

The country's economy has been causing anxiety since several years but lately it has deteriorated rapidly. Signs of recession had started showing in the beginning of 1956. With the cessation of foreign aid and imports during the war with Pakistan, industries whose production was dependent on imported raw materials and spare parts from abroad were seriously affected. But at that time the country was psychologically prepared to face such adversity. As a result programmes of import substitution were undertaken on a large scale and a feeling of confidence took roots that the country was all set on the way to self-sufficiency. But even before these efforts could bear fruit, the Government succumbed to foreign pressure and devalued the Rupee. Relying on the Rs. 750 crores untied foreign loans available, it liberalised imports. This policy adversely affected the trade and industry of the country.

The quantum of foreign loans increased, so did the prices, but the pace of industrial production did not grow. In some industries, production for 1966 was even less than that for 1965. The object of export promotion also was not realised. The balance of payment position on trade account for 1966-67 shows an adverse balance of Rs. 773.4 crores, which is higher than that for the preceding year. In the sphere of foreign trade the same trend still persists. Devaluation thus has done harm to our economy.

It appears, however, that in spite of this; international forces are exerting once again to impose on us yet another dose of devaluation. By threatening to resign if anything of that sort to happens, Deputy Prime Minister Shri Morarji Desi has given an indication of firmness. But unless those basic ills are remedied which account for an adverse balance of payment position, and which compel us to approach foreign governments with a begging bowl, it may not be possible to sustain even the present value of the Rupee.

Ad Hocism Will Not Do

Comprehensive measures are called for to counter the effects of growing recession and to impart dynamism to the economy. It is a matter of regret that the Government does not seem to appreciate the gravity of the situation and has made little effort to analyze it carefully. A casual consideration of problems and adoption of *ad hoc* measures only to solve them will not do. The devaluation decision of June 1966 was based on the analysis that the slump in economy had been caused by paucity of imported raw materials. And in this year's budget this aspect has been ignored, and drought and shortfall in agricultural production have been blamed for the economic crisis. Then, some engineering industries are sought to be kept alive with the assistance of executive orders from the Railway Department. There is no realisation of the fact that with a halt in the expansion programme of Railways these orders would only mean needless waste.

Diversionary Tactics

When today the situation demands some revolutionary changes in the country's economic policy, the Congress

Government at the Centre is wasting much of its time and energy on issues which may be important by themselves but which are not relevant so far as the basic problems of Indian economy are concerned. Thus, the problem of privy purses, the issues raised by the Hazari Report, the proposal for nationalization of banks and general insurance are animatedly debated, and projected as if the economic development of the country hinges round these questions. Actually, these questions are not even remotely connected with our basic problems of food scarcity, falling production, growing unemployment and risible prices. And when these matters are debated over and over again, with Government giving no indication of a will to clinch these, issues, one is naturally led to suspect that the real object of these discussions is only to divert public attention from the crucial problems and use these debates to exert political pressure on certain sections.

Social Controls of Banks

At the last session of Parliament, Finance Minister Shri Morarji Desai made a statement that an Enquiry Commission would be appointed to go into the problems of banking. This statement also announced a scheme for social control of banks. As the Finance Minister evidently held that the problems of banking merited a thorough examination by a Commission, wish he had waited for the Commission's report before precipitately coming forth with his Social Control Scheme. The real problem today is of capital formation, and social control is not going to help capital formation. Also, it is doubtful that this scheme would ensure optimum utilization of the resources available with banks. There is no doubt that agriculture and to small industries need capital badly. But what about the industries that are benefiting today from these resources? How will they run? Or, are they regarded as unnecessary? The proposal to have representatives of small industry and agriculture on the Board of Directors is welcome. But how are they going to be selected? Are they to be nominated? If so, the nominations are very likely to be vitiated by political consideration. I wonder why depositors have been given no representation on the Board. Besides, foreign banks have been kept outside the purview of this scheme. This would naturally injure the interest of Indian banks. It would be better if instead of launching such political schemes, the Government decided to open new banks to meet the growing demand for capital investment.

No Plan Holiday

We have been disappointed also with the Planning Commission. By suggesting that the Fourth Five Year Plan should commence from April 1, 1969, it has agreed to a Plan Holiday. The situation calls for greater endeavour and not a holiday. When conditions are difficult, well-considered, planned measures become all the more necessary. Programmes should be undertaken to remove the strains and cracks caused in the country's economy as a result of the Plans till now, and in a way so as to avail of our developed potential. The present recession and large-scale educated unemployment owe to a great extent to the manner in which Plans have been arbitrarily slashed or changed during the past two years. Productive schemes under the Plan have been cut while unproductive expenditure of the administration has been increasing. Such budgeting is not conducive to economic growth. Recession leads to fall in revenues and increase in administrative expenditures causes inflation. As a consequence, despite all efforts, deficit financing becomes unavoidable. In this matter, however, let us be practical and not doctrinaire. In order to utilise the potential of the unemployed, and to implement quick yielding schemes, a judicious recourse to deficit financing would certainly prove profitable.

The Planning Commission should play the role of an expert and suggest short-term and long-term measures to solve the problems which face us today. Planning does not mean a mere fixation of targets in various spheres and an arithmetical dovetailing of these targets. It calls for imagination, farsight, and a sense of realism-qualities, which unfortunately have been conspicuous by their absence in the preceding Plans.

We Must Be Self-Reliant

A constant refrain heard nowadays is about paucity of resources. I do not accept that this nation lacks resources. There are adequate resources in this country–human, physical and financial. What is required is that the size and shape of the Plan should be correlated to the quantum of available and potential resources. Till now our Plans have been based on foreign resources, foreign machinery, foreign technicians, foreign capital and lately, even foreign raw materials and market. Schemes are formulated to secure what we do not possess, but no attention is paid to the conservation of what we, already have, or to develop up that basis. Agriculture and indigenous industry have been neglected, and foreign collaboration has been welcomed even when the terms of agreement are contrary to our interests and derogatory to our self-respect. Vested foreign interests in this country are today so powerful that they seek not only to influence our economic programmes, but our educational and political policies as well. If independence is to be preserved, we must become self-reliant in the economic sphere. This must be the cornerstone of our future plans.

Problems of Agriculture

Repeatedly for the past many years we are being treated to pronouncements that priority would be given to agriculture. But the Government's policies evince little regard either for the farmer's interests, or the needs of agriculture. Prices of fertilizers in India are the highest in the world. Under this head, Government had given an assistance of Rs. 55 crores last year.

But in this year's Central budget, this subsidy has been stopped. Foreign concerns have been permitted to set up fertilizer units here and they have been allowed to fix fertilizer prices arbitrarily. Fact is that if the farmer was enabled to meet his fuel requirements with soft coke, and encouraged to use cow-dung as manure, there would be no need of any new fertilizer factories. A report of the National Council for Applied Economic Research has noted: 'India burns ten Sindries every year!' But, indifferent to this indigenous potential, we continue to hanker after foreign concerns.

The manners in which some districts have been selected for intensive cultivation betray a partisan approach. All told, the programme is not going to achieve its objective of maximum production. Also, the use of fertilizers, to the exclusion of natural manure, will gravely affect the fertility of the soil. One shudders to contemplate the possibility that a day may arrive as the result of our present myopic policies when rich abundant areas like Ludhiana and Panjore may become barren. Let us avert such a calamity.

No doubt, some attention has been paid to irrigation, but the Government's ways of doing things are such that the general reaction of farmers could be summed up by the Hindi saying: ***Ka barakha jab krishi sukhani*** (of what avail the water provided only after the crops have failed). In the matter of inter-state river water disputes provincial loyalties have become so strong that crores of cusecs of water are allowed to go waste into the ocean rather than that the parties to the dispute relent a bit. The decision to provide power for tube-wells at the rate of 12 paise per unit is commendable, but the decision can have meaning only if power is actually made available to them.

Agriculture and Price Policy

Procurement schemes of Government have hit the farmers very badly. Kerala has proved the worst offender on this count. Here we have *babus* in the offices determining how much grain a particular peasant must produce and how much he should consume. And the peasant is ordered to deposit his entire surplus with the Government godowns. The prices of various crops fixed by the Centre are uneconomic. While it is essential that prices should be stabilized, it would be unjust, and suicidal besides, to deny the farmer a fair and full price for his produce. The foremost object of our price policy should be to prevent a fall in the income of producers, specially primary producers. After all, it is agricultural income which sustains the economy.

It is true that rise in the price of foodgrains has caused great difficulty to the urban population-particularly the low and fixed income groups. For these sections, essential commodities of life should be made available at fair prices. If the Madras Government can successfully implement in some cities its scheme to sell rice at a Rupee per measure, there is no reason why similar steps should not be possible in other parts of the country. Also, dearness allowance must be linked with the cost of living. It is regrettable that the Government refuses to accept this principle. This attitude of it's the cause of many a dispute and of industrial unrest. Apart from workers and employees, pensioners also must be paid dearness allowances, and their pensions should be co-related with present pay scales.

Scrap Food Zones

Food Zones and the very many restrictions imposed on the movement of various commodities are economically unsound and also against the spirit of the Constitution. These restrictions block normal channels of trade, create an artificial scarcity in the market, and encourage smuggling and black-marketing. This policy militates against national integration also. If we cannot think about as vital a matter as food from the national standpoint, and allow our vision to be warped by narrow regional interests, national integration would become a meaningless slogan. It seems that some corrupt officials, power-hungry politicians and big businessmen who find smuggling a very lucrative trade have developed so great a vested interest in the continuance of this policy that mere logic and reasoning if not going to change it.

Need for National Approach

In the absence of a national approach to economic problems, of proper planning, concerted effort and sound leadership at the Centre, every state and section is exerting to fend for itself with total unconcern about the rest. As they say: 'Every one for himself, and let the Devil take the hindmost.' Wittingly or unwittingly this attitude has been encouraging provincialism. When Kerala's Chief Minister Shri E.M.S. Namboodripad advances claims that he should be allowed to use the foreign exchange earned out of exports from Kerala to buy foodgrains from abroad for his State, or when he calls for a Kerala Bandh against the Centre, it's surely a blow struck at the country's unity. Similarly, when on the plea of securing justice for the Maharashtrians, the Shiv Sena agitates against any quarter being given to people from other States in the services or trades of Bombay; it is becoming blind to a basic fact, namely, that the economic interests of all sections in the country are inseverly interlinked. Unemployment and poverty in this country can be eradicated only by a combined effort.

Inter-State Disputes

In the resolution of the country's political problems also, this basic unity of the nation must never be overlooked. Today, there are border disputes between some States. These should be generally settled on the basis of principles formulated at the time of reorganization of States. The Jana Sangh accepts that language is one of the factors which should be taken into consideration while demarcating the borders of two States, but it does not consider it the sole determinant. Language has an important place in administration, particularly in a democratic administration. Therefore, ordinarily, linguistic boundaries have crystallized into State boundaries. But there are people who would like language to be the one and exclusive factor to be taken into account. The approach of these people often smacks of a sub-national loyalty. The Jana Sangh disapproves of it.

The Mahajan Commission had been appointed to report on the Mysore-Maharashtra and Mysore-Kerala border disputes. The Commission's report should no doubt help settle the disputes. But this is possible only if there is a readiness to consider the issue dispassionately and without any sense of false prestige. The suggestions for an opinion poll cannot be accepted. Demarcation of State boundaries is the function of Parliament.

Reorganisation of Assam

The Central leadership's handling of the issue of Assam's reorganisation has greatly complicated it. Home Minister Chavan's statement just before the General Election that Assam would be given a federal structure was a political blunder which the Centre is finding it hard to rectify now. Unfortunately, the seeds of separatism in Assam were sown when a special place was given to Assam's Hill Tribes in the Sixth Schedule if the Constitution. Today, we are having to reap its ill-fruits. Creation of a separate Naga State for a population of just three lakh has greatly encouraged these separatist trends. And foreign missionaries in the region have been doing their worst to incite disruptive forces. Our Assam policy ought to take cognisance of all these aspects of the problem: mere patchwork will not do.

Why Not the Hindu Nagas?

The Government has been holding prolonged negotiation with the underground Nagas, but no fruitful outcome is yet in sight. Meanwhile, it has been reported that these rebel Nagas are hobnobbing with Communist China. Outbursts of sporadic violence also have continued. Manipur particularly has seen an intensification of such activity. Obviously, the extremist section is availing of the present interlude only to prepare for a bigger revolt. The Government of India must be extremely vigilant. It should consciously exert to isolate the rebels and deal with them sternly. It would be in place to mention here that half the population of State comprises of Hindu Nagas. New Delhi's dialogue with Nagaland till now has been exclusively through the medium of the Baptist Mission. The Hindu tribes have never been given the recognition due to them. Their must change. Their interests and rights also must be safeguarded.

No Going Back on Kashmir

Following the removal of restrictions on Mirza Afzal Beg, and Sheikh Abdullah's release in Delhi, those elements have once again become active who would like to detach Kashmir from India. All the stale arguments, long debunked and exploded, are being repeated again, and proposals are being revived which have been rejected by the people as against national interest or impractical. The Central Government's support for these proposals is being canvassed on the plea that these would procure us Pakistan's friendship. It is high time now that all these self-anointed patrons of peace and justice, as wells as Pakistan itself and the international powers who keep giving us uncalled for counsel about Kashmir were told in plain, unambiguous language that Kashmir is an indivisible part and parcel of India, and, come what may, there was going to be no compromise about it. In this matter, we cannot allow any intervention even by the UNO or any agency of its.

Some people have been advocating even greater autonomy for Kashmir than it now enjoys. The proposal is rooted in separatism and runs counter to national interest and our Constitution. We would like to state categorically that the people of India will not suffer any act which amounts to reversing the process of

Kashmir's fuller integration with India. In this context, I would like to say a word about Article 370. Though this is an internal arrangement of ours, and does not in any way affect the fact that Kashmir is an integral part of India, it is certainly an exceptional provision which ought to be abrogated. Its repeal would serve a valuable psychological purpose. A11 speculations about Kashmir would automatically stop.

Failure of Sadiq Government

The Centre should also pay attention to the internal administration of Jammu and Kashmir State. Shri Sadiq has failed to give to the state a clean, impartial and strong administration.

The indifference, apathy and communal bias betrayed by the J&K police in its handling of the case in which a Hindu girl was abducted and forcibly married has impaired the faith of Kashmiri Hindus in the administration. The Hindus of the Valley complain that Union Home Minister Shri Chavan also has failed to fulfil his assurances. It is regrettable that any section should feel that they are being denied justice, or that they are insecure. A Commission headed by Shri Gajendragadkar, former Chief Justice of the Supreme Court, has been constituted to examine the question of representation in service etc. Misgivings about discrimination on regional grounds must certainly be enquired into, but it would be against the letter and spirit of the Constitution if the issue is looked at from the communal angle.

Vested Interests in Riots

There have been during recent month's communal disturbances in some parts of the country. These are unfortunate and deplorable. So far as Government is concerned, it must deal with all such breaches of peace and incidents of rioting sternly and impartially. But I must say that the code which regulates the administration's policy and conduct on such occasions is the one that was evolved during the British regime. It did not aim at curbing the mischievous elements or punishing the guilty. The Government would conspicuously appear to hold the scales even between the communities involved while in fact its actions only perpetuated the gulf between the communities. This code of make-believe impartiality must change, and rioters, to whichever community they belong, should be punished.

There are elements in the country who have developed a vested political interest in riots. Instead of exerting to localize vested these incidents and suppressing them, these elements deliberately magnify and distort reports about these incidents in a manner as to suit their purpose. Whatever the incident and whatever the place of occurrence, theirs is a stereotyped analysis; and a set line of propaganda. According to them, it is the Muslims who are killed everywhere and the killers always are workers of the Bharatiya Jana Sangh and the R.S.S. Amusingly, even at places where the Jana Sangh and the R.S.S. do not exist, journals belonging to these sections discover 'strongholds' of these organizations. Their conduct often reminds you of the technique of pick pockets and thieves who act in a concerted manner and after a crime has been successfully committed by one of them, rush in a certain direction shouting '*Chor*! *Chor!*' and start belabouring some innocent passerby. By then, the real thief would have decamped. We have certainly to be very careful about these elements.

Language

Both patriotism as well as common sense demand that the country's work should be conducted in its own languages. The Central Education Ministry's decision this year to make Indian languages the media of education right up to the University level is a commendable step. The decision conforms to the recommendations of the Education Commission. The Parliamentary Committee on Education, the Education Ministers Conference and the Conference of Vice-Chancellors also have endorsed and supported the decision. In spite of this, some Anglophiles are attacking this decision. The problems they refer to are either imaginary, or affect isolated individuals, or then, pertain to the transitional period only. It would be better if instead of raising this hullabaloo about problems, they exerted earnestly to solve them. After the formation of non-Congress Governments in several States, the use of regional languages at the State level has considerably increased. If the pace is maintained, within a few months the work of Government in most of these States would be conducted in the people's languages. I must congratulate all these Governments for giving the country's languages their due place. By pursuing this policy, they have justified their claim of being popular Governments.

The Central Government's policy in regard to the replacement of English by Hindi at the Centre has continued to create difficulties. It is a matter of regret that instead of taking positive steps in this direction, the Government by its actions has only been creating controversies and misgiving. The Jana Sangh does not support any step which restricts the right of those who do not know Hindi or deprives them of any of their rights. The Jana Sangh has, therefore, been demanding that all examinations of the U.P.S.C. should be conducted through the media of regional languages and that knowledge of any particular language should not be compulsory at the time of recruitment. Those who want to use English during the period of transition should be permitted to do so. But the perpetual domination of English and denial to Hindi of its rightful place cannot be suffered. The Official Languages (Amendment), Bill and the language resolution recently passed are steps in the wrong direction. The Centre's language policy as envisaged by this Bill will be an impediment in the way of even those State Governments which want to carry on their work in their regional languages. So long as English continues to rule in New Delhi, Tamil also will not be able to get its rightful place in Madras.

U.A.R. Must Ponder

The foreign policy of the Government of India neither reflects public opinion nor does it protect national interest. Government's attitude towards the West Asian war, for instance, did not have the approval of the people. When Britain had bombed the Suez Canal, the people of India had protested strongly against it. We have always favoured friendship with the Arab countries. But when the Indo-Pak war broke out, we failed to get even lip sympathy from the Arab countries, even though Pakistan was obviously in the wrong. Jordon actually pleaded Pakistan's case against India. The Indian people then felt greatly disappointed with the Arabs. It was this disappointment which explains the change in their attitude during the Israel–U.A.R. conflict. If the Arab countries sincerely desire India's friendship, they must appreciate our feelings. They must also realize that when they can have warm relations with our enemies, there is no reason why we should not have relations with Israel.

Sino-Pak Collusion

Our policy towards Communist China and Pakistan should be such as befits a self-respecting nation dealing with enemy countries who have aggressed on her soil. It is surprising that we have not yet recognized the Government of Formosa. Also, India must actively contribute to Tibet's struggle for independence. Our present attitude towards the Dalai Lama obstructs, rather than helps, fulfillment of this objective. Pakistan has virtually thrown the Tashkent Agreement into the waste paper basket. It is ridiculous that our leaders should nevertheless continue to swear by it. There is an obvious shift in Soviet Russia's policy towards Pakistan. It seems that our attitude to Pakistan is determined mainly by an intention to please the Soviet leaders. We really see no other explanation for Prime Minister Shrimati Indira Gandhi's uncalled for congratulatory message to Ayub Khan in respect of the Mangla Dam. If India's policy towards Pakistan is to be formulated not on the basis of that country's own conduct but in deference to the wishes of either Soviet Russia or America, there can never be peace in this region.

China and Pakistan are preparing a concerted plan of aggression. We cannot remain indifferent to the scheme they are hatching. No doubt, there has been some increase lately in our military preparation but much more needs to be done to meet the requirements of the situation. China has made great progress in the sphere of nuclear armament. The Government of India, however, continues to stick obtusely to its original stand. I would like to reiterate our view that India must go in for the nuclear bomb. Our failure to take this decision gravely endangers our security.

Peking-Pindi Patriots

In the context of this threat posed by China and Pakistan, we must also consider the activities of elements within the country who take ideological inspiration from them and act in concert with their designs. In West Bengal and Kerala, after securing representation in Government, the Mao Communists have been feeling greatly emboldened and have been misusing power to promote their designs. By organizing the Naxalbari uprising they subverted law and order. Simultaneously they have been trying to paralyze the administration and demoralize the police.

The country must be ever watchful. People must ensure that these elements are not allowed to create a situation which could be taken advantage of by Communist China or Pakistan. Whenever and wherever these elements disturb peace or pose a threat to the country's security they should be ruthlessly suppressed. But it is necessary that these forces be checkmated on the political level also. The people of this country have an abiding faith in nationalism and democracy and they will not tolerate elements who seek to subvert these values.

However, the powers assumed by the Central Government under the Unlawful Activities Prevention Act recently passed are unjustified, and unwarranted. It appears that following its defeat in the last election, the Congress Government at the Centre is anxious to give to itself all such power as might some day come handy to it to retain its stranglehold on Government.

Channelise Popular Awakening

We should also be cautious about people who see in every popular agitation the hidden hand of Communists and suggest that the agitation must be crushed. In the changing situation at present, public agitations are natural and even essential. In fact, they are the media and expressions of social awakening. It is of course necessary that these agitations should be made instruments of a constructive revolution and not allowed to become violent or adventurist. Therefore, we must actively participate in popular movements, and try to guide them. Those who are keen to preserve the *status quo* in the economic and social spheres feel unnerved by these movements and are wont to create an atmosphere of despair and pessimism. We are sorry we cannot cooperate with them. We think these sections are trying in vain to halt the wheels of progress and avert the destiny of the country. This is not possible.

While we do draw inspiration from the past, we do not regard the past as the highest pinnacle of our achievement; while we have a realistic approach to the present, we do not feel tied down even to the present; and while we do have before our eyes a vision of a great future for this country, we are not mere visionaries but are *karmayogis* resolved to translate our vision into reality.

We are pledged to the service not of any particular community or section but of the entire nation. Every countryman is blood of our blood and flesh of our flesh. We shall not rest till we are able to give to every one of them a sense of pride that they are children of *Bharatmata*. We shall make Mother India *sujala suphala* (laden with fruits and overflowing with water) in the real sense of these words. As *Dashapraharana Dharini Durga* (Goddess Durga with her ten weapons) she would be able to vanquish evil; as Lakshmi she would be able to disburse prosperity all over and as Saraswati she would dispel the gloom of ignorance and spread the radiance of knowledge all around her. With faith in ultimate victory, let us dedicate ourselves to this task.

VANDE MATARAM

(XIV Annual Session of Bharatiya Jana Sangh)

□

Bibliography

Online:

https://en.wikipedia.org/wiki/Deendayal_Upadhyaya

http://deendayalupadhyaya.org

blog.lkadvani.in

Books:

Bhishikar, C. P., *Concept of Rashtra*.

Deodhar, V. N., *A Profile*.

Jog, B. N., *Politics for Nation's Sake*.

Kelkar, B. K., *Political Thought*.

Kulkarni, S. A., *Integral Economic Policy*.

Nene, V. V., *Integral Humanism*.

Thengadi, D. B., *An Inquest*.

□

Index